What Happened in Craig

Alaska's Worst Unsolved Mass Murder

Epicenter Press

Epicenter Press is a regional press publishing nonfiction books about the arts, history, environment, and diverse cultures and lifestyles of Alaska and the Pacific Northwest.
For more information, visit www.EpicenterPress.com

Text © 2018 Leland E. Hale
www.LelandHale.com

Cover and interior design: Aubrey Anderson

ISBN: 978-1-941890-22-6 (Trade Paperback)
ISBN: 978-1-941890-19-6 (Ebook)

Library of Congress Control Number: 2018949827

10 9 8 7 6 5 4 3 2 1

What Happened in Craig

in Craig

Alaska's Worst Unsolved Mass Murder

Leland E. Hale

Epicenter Press
Kenmore, WA

In Memory of
Walter J. Gilmour

Dedicated to
All who suffered through this tragedy

Author's Note

This is a work of nonfiction. While most of the dialogue in it is taken directly from court and police transcripts, there are multiple instances in which it has been reconstructed on the basis of the author's interviews with relevant individuals. In addition, certain scenes have been dramatically recreated to more effectively portray the personalities involved in this story and the atmosphere surrounding the events upon which this book is based.

It should be emphasized that a police investigation and criminal trial produce conflicting versions of events. Where such conflict exists, the author has sought to provide the version which, in his view, is most credible.

Part One

The *Investor* in May 1982, with Mark Coulthurst at the bow. The *Casino* is behind and to the right of the Investor. (Courtesy of Doug McNair.)

Mark Coulthurst in May, 1982. (Courtesy of Doug McNair.)

Ruth Ann's restaurant in Craig, Alaska, where the Coulthurst family ate their last supper. (Courtesy of Leland Hale.)

Alaska State Trooper composite sketches of the skiffman seen leaving the *Investor* in the days after the murders. (Courtesy of the Alaska State Troopers.)

John Peel in August, 1991. (Courtesy of the *Bellingham Herald*.)

Hill Bar in downtown Criag, Alaska. This bar was frequented by John Peel and the *Libby 8* crew. (Courtesy of Leland Hale.)

1

Craig, Alaska
Tuesday, September 7, 1982

The CF/V *Investor* had lain at anchor for a day, enshrouded in the fog off Fish Egg Island. The weather lifted by mid-morning but still she lay there, bobbing gently in the shallow waters of Ben's Cove. By late afternoon, she was on fire.

The smoke rising from her hull—thin and gray at first, becoming a thick black plume as the fire caught hold—was visible for miles. When the first mayday went out folks started scrambling: on shore, they rushed for anything that floated and had a motor; at sea, boats began to converge from all directions, closing in on a spot one-quarter mile south of Cole Island.

By the time the first boats arrived, the living quarters of the *Investor* were fully engulfed by the blaze; bright orange flames filled her wheelhouse, tongues of fire ripped out of her stateroom, out of her cabin, out of her head. A dense cloud swirled around the vessel, fed by the inferno that roared beneath it.

"There's no way we can get on the boat and accomplish anything," reasoned the skipper of the troller *Casino*, the first boat on the scene. The fire was so intense and so hot that he feared to take his boat closer than fifty feet. He had three full propane tanks on the stern of his boat and he didn't want them to explode. With the tide starting to turn, he was also afraid of running aground. When a small skiff arrived a few minutes later, *Casino* skipper Bruce Anderson asked its operator to do what he couldn't.

"Circle the boat and look for survivors," he told him. The skiff made several loops around the purse seiner, but saw nothing except a few, unidentifiable objects floating in the water.[1]

The fire, meanwhile, continued to spread. The flames in the wheelhouse began to melt the roof, the fire in the cabin blossomed toward the stem of the boat, creeping past the hatch and along the deck to the seine net. Within fifteen minutes, the entire back deck was ablaze. Lacking any way to fight the fire the boats stood by helpless.

While everyone else hesitated, Alaska State Trooper Bob Anderson rushed to the scene. At 4:20 p.m. that day, Ketchikan dispatch had relayed a call from the Coast Guard, telling him a boat was on fire outside Craig, seven miles from his office in Klawock. Beyond that, information was sketchy. As Anderson sped south on the gravel-paved Craig-Klawock highway, however, he gained firsthand information: what he saw was a large vessel, close by the northeastern tip of Fish Egg Island and totally consumed by flames. The newness of the boat, and the fact that it was the end of the season, told Anderson everything he needed to know. The boat's owner probably hadn't done well that season. The seiner was likely being torched for the insurance money.

In Craig, Anderson searched desperately for firefighting equipment. His first stop was the police station, but the Craig Police Department was newly formed and lacked a firefighting vessel. From the police station, Anderson rushed to the fire department and then to the Forest Service—but again he was out of luck: some of the pumps didn't work, and the pumps that did work couldn't be connected to the hoses he found. By themselves, neither the pumps nor the hoses were capable of putting out a book of matches, much less a fully involved vessel fire.

Rather than continuing to waste time in Craig, Anderson commandeered a 26-foot boat owned by the Alaska Fish and Wildlife Protection Service. He was headlong on his way to the fire scene, but didn't get far. The boat's batteries were dead; it wouldn't start. Anderson sprinted to his personal boat, which, luckily, was moored nearby.

When Anderson arrived at the fire, a small flotilla was standing by. The day was overcast; winds were from the south at ten miles per hour;

---

1   A purse seiner is a fishing vessel that uses a seine net to catch fish. Once a school of fish is located, the net is deployed as a wall around them by a smaller boat, called a power skiff, which tows the net out from the mother ship. A lead line on the net is then pulled in, "pursing" the net closed on the bottom, preventing fish from escaping by swimming downward.

the seas were calm. The fire was raging out of control; flames had now overtaken the entire cabin, bridge, wheelhouse, and galley, as well as the seine net on the stern. Anderson quickly learned that firefighting efforts up to that time had been limited to the valiant efforts of one man, who had managed to unhook the boat's anchor and tow it closer to shore. Anderson tried to convince a large fish-packing vessel to move alongside the boat and douse the flames with its wash-down pumps. The skipper refused. He was afraid to get too close.

Anderson was in an unenviable position: the situation was growing worse with each minute, but he couldn't do anything. The fire was so relentless that the boat began to fall in on itself. The roof of the wheelhouse finally collapsed and the fiberglass walls of the cabin began to melt; the mast started to fold away from its base and, eventually, was torn from the deck by its own weight and fell into the water.

When the tug *Andy Head* steamed to the scene at quarter to six that evening, Trooper Anderson again asked for help. Although the tug had only one pump, it was better than nothing. Trooper Anderson talked her skipper into backing in as close to the *Investor* as they felt safe. In no time, she'd managed to put out the fire on the seine net. That accomplished, she turned her hose to the boat's cabin—which proved considerably more difficult to extinguish. So difficult that the tug's skipper called the Coast Guard and requested that firefighting pumps be airlifted to the scene.

In the meantime, several creative attempts were made to put out the fire. None were more creative than the attempt made by a tugboat named *The Spruce*, which tried to push the *Investor* on its side, roll it into the salt water and kill the flames. But her efforts only succeeded in pushing the *Investor* closer to shore, where she finally hit bottom. Nudged by the outgoing tide, the still burning vessel started to list on her starboard side.

Trooper Anderson had seen enough. He returned to Craig. Once there he called his boss, Sergeant John Glass, in Ketchikan. The *Investor* fire, he told him, was no accident. From witness descriptions, he knew the fire had spread quickly, had exploded with reckless fury, and a fire like that bore all the earmarks of arson. Sergeant Glass immediately agreed to send a trooper arson investigator to the scene. He couldn't promise whether anyone would arrive before the next day.

On shore, Anderson also tried to learn what he could about the burning boat. The owner/operator of the *Investor*, he discovered, was Mark Coulthurst of Blaine, Washington; Coulthurst had been fishing out of Petersburg, Alaska, with his pregnant wife and two children, Johnny and Kimberly. Word was that Irene Coulthurst and the children had returned to Washington State so their daughter, Kimberly, could start school. The Coast Guard and the Craig police were both trying to confirm the whereabouts of the family. Anderson was also told that Craig police had located a power skiff parked at the cold storage dock and that it had been seen coming from the direction of the fire.

At 7:30 that evening, a Temsco Airlines helicopter arrived at the fire scene, bearing several firefighting pumps from the Coast Guard base in Ketchikan. As the pumps were offloaded onto the *Andy Head*, there was new hope of putting out the fire. Not long afterwards, Trooper Anderson received a radio call in Craig. The *Andy Head* had managed to subdue the fire. As they had brought it under control, however, they had found something suspicious. Something that might have been used to set the fire. Trooper Anderson agreed to return to the scene.

Back at Ben's Cove, Anderson found the *Investor* reduced to a smoldering hull. The cabin and wheelhouse had completely collapsed and, because the boat was made of fiberglass, were layered on top of each other like a burnt sandwich. On top of that hulk, one of the firefighters had found a metal pail that looked like it could have been used to carry an accelerant. Anderson soon determined that the pail had other origins. On seine boats, a pail is often kept in the wheelhouse, where it stores the sponges and mops used to scrub down the decks. As the walls of the *Investor's* upper deck caved in, Anderson reasoned, the pail had innocently found its way to the lower deck.

Trooper Anderson's cursory inspection of the pail brought him to another conclusion: the fire, he decided, had cooled sufficiently to allow inspection. The trooper put on the heavy gloves and boots he had borrowed from a nearby seiner and clambered aboard the sagging vessel. Behind him were three volunteers. His watch read eight o'clock in the evening; fully four hours had passed since the fire began. This late in the year, the days had grown shorter in southeast Alaska, although a lingering dusk hung in the sky.

On board the *Investor*, the trooper and his helpers found themselves walking on a slippery, dangerous mess. The burned areas—now an ugly black mixture of charcoal and melted fiberglass—were slick from the water that had been used to fight the fire and spongy from the effects of the blaze. The boat itself was listing twenty degrees toward starboard, which made it difficult to move without falling. Each time they lifted a layer of fiberglass to investigate, the sudden blast of oxygen caused a flare-up. The trooper eventually burned a hole through his rubber boots. In the back of his mind was another worry: the risk of exploding fuel tanks; "still," he thought, "the fuel tanks surely would have gone by now if they were going to blow."

Anderson's intent was to conduct a preliminary probe, to see what he could uncover before night overtook them. He knew a full investigation would have to wait until daylight and, besides, he wanted to leave the bulk of the investigation to the arson experts. One of the volunteers, however, had gone into an area where the galley door would have been. As he did so, something oozed up between a space in the fiberglass matting and other debris on the deck. The volunteer thought it looked like "some warm gel-like substance like you would see the gelatin from like a cherry pie filling that you would get out of a can." The man quickly called his discovery to the trooper's attention. Anderson knelt to take a closer look and decided it was a dog or deer carcass of some sort.

"It isn't very big," he thought. "It looks like a deer laying on its side with the legs sticking straight out and totally unrecognizable, with just burnt tissue and some gut material hanging out." On closer examination, Anderson reached a different conclusion. He realized that he was looking at a human body—a human body that had been burned almost beyond recognition. Only seconds later, a second volunteer lifted another layer of fiberglass, just past the spot where the fishing boat's stack had been. He discovered yet another body. Now everything had changed.

By law, Trooper Anderson could not remove either of the bodies without permission of the coroner, but he was loath to broadcast his macabre discovery over the airwaves. He radioed the Ketchikan coroner and communicated his request in the tersest language he could find. "Found two, maybe more," he said. "Permission to remove."

Twenty minutes later, he got a call from the Coast Guard. "Permission to proceed."

Anderson and two of the volunteers returned to the place where the second body was found. Immediately upon lifting that body they found another, directly beneath it; the two victims had been thrust against each other in a gruesome post-mortem dance that put the head of one at the feet of the other. Unlike the first body they had found, however, these two were not burned as badly and were recognizably human. The one on top was an adult male, large framed with short hair. A perforation in his cranium suggested gunshot wound. The bottom body was also that of an adult, but with longer hair and a more rounded body. The form suggested it was a woman.

Anderson now turned his attention to the port side of the *Investor*, where the cabin wall had caved in. He thought he'd seen something while they were digging out the two bodies that were stacked together. Locked beneath a morass of twisted and bubbled fiberglass—in what was once the skipper's stateroom—were the remains of what was "either a baby or a very small child, very unrecognizable." Only with great difficulty did they manage to remove the remains. Not only had the wall fallen over, it had been pushed up, so that it formed a wedge around the young victim. With night fast approaching, Anderson called off the search for additional victims; the body count was now at four.

With some difficulty—the smaller bodies were fragile and pieces of tissue fell off when they were handled—Anderson and his associates placed the four bodies in body bags. From there, they were taken to the cannery dock at Columbia Ward Fisheries in Craig. A small crowd gathered to watch the proceedings.

The removal process was tedious. Because the tide was at its lowest ebb, the only way to take the bodies off the boat was to place them on pallet boards and lift them out with a crane. From there, the remains were lowered onto a cart, rolled into a warehouse and placed under lock and key. Dead tired, Trooper Anderson was ready to return home. The hour was close to midnight.

Before he could leave, however, Anderson was intercepted by a Craig policeman. The officer told him he had a witness, someone who had seen an individual coming from the fire scene in a power skiff, just after the fire was spotted. The witness also had seen the skiff operator tie up the skiff at the cold storage dock.

"Can we set up an appointment in the morning?" Trooper Anderson asked wearily.

"He's going back to college," the officer replied. "He's leaving on the first flight tomorrow."

Trooper Anderson made his way to the bunkhouse of the E.C. Phillips cold storage facility. The young man he met there said he'd been on his way to the fire when his boat ran out of gas. What he had witnessed still seemed strange to him. "The fire had just been announced and it seemed like everyone else was headed out toward the fire," the cold storage employee told the trooper. "Except this skiff. This skiff was headed in the opposite direction, toward the dock, and the guy in it seemed like he could care less about the fire."

Asked to describe the man, the witness said he had brown or blonde hair and was wearing a baseball hat. He thought the hat had an emblem on front, like an Alaska pipeline or California Fish and Game hat. He thought the guy was wearing glasses and guessed the skiffman's age to be near his own, twenty or 21. He estimated his weight at 150 pounds, but couldn't be sure because the skiffman was sitting down when he saw him. Still, he'd gotten a pretty good look, their boats having passed within ten yards of each other.

After the interview, Trooper Anderson went to the dock and looked at the skiff. He examined it briefly and determined that the rain—which had returned with a vengeance—made it impossible to fingerprint. He decided to leave it where it was; the hour was late and besides, even if he did seize it, he had no place to keep it. After his long day at Ben's Cove, Anderson didn't realize that he was staring at the *Investor's* power skiff.[2] As far as he knew, the skiff was significant only because it had been seen coming from the fire. Anderson left the cold storage dock, called Sergeant Glass in Ketchikan, and briefed him on the day's activities. After making sure that someone from the Craig police department was available to secure the crime scene, he went home.

---

2   With a heavy seine net that's a quarter mile long, fishermen need a powerful boat to tow it away from the mother ship, and then hold it taut as the fish start pooling. The power skiff, with its high horsepower engine, lives up to its name as it repeats that task over and over during the fishing season.

On the drive back to Klawock, Anderson tried to pull everything together. He had expected a crime scene, but not this, not what he had found. All he could think was how bizarre it was: the sights, the smells, the devastation. How could he describe what it was like to find a baby's body? The experience gnawed at him. Anderson had two kids of his own; he wanted to get home and hug them; he wanted to sleep next to his wife and disassociate himself from the *Investor*. This night—and many nights into the future—he would have nightmares about what he had seen.

2

Craig, Alaska

Two days earlier, *Investor* skipper Mark Coulthurst was at Ruth Ann's, Craig's finest restaurant, with his wife and children. After an intense month of near nonstop fishing, it was finally time to let loose a little. They had plenty of reasons to celebrate: it was Mark's 28th birthday; the next day Irene and the kids were heading back to Washington State for the start of the new school year; the salmon fishing season was near at its end.

Though Mark enforced a no drinking rule on the fishing grounds, that night at Ruth Ann's was different: they would have a round of drinks, a great meal, and maybe another round of drinks, or two. No matter that Mark had to borrow a $100 from another fisherman to pay their bill. He was good for it. They'd caught over 100,000 salmon that season; even at depressed prices, that was a lot of dough.

By most measures, though, Mark was an unlikely fisherman. He looked more like a high school shop teacher, with his thick thatch of dark hair and horn-rimmed glasses. In contrast to the Scandinavians and Alaska Natives who made up a big part of the Alaskan fishery, he did not come from a long line of professional fisher folk. His dad, "Big John" Coulthurst—while a larger than life personality—was a maintenance supervisor at the Whatcom County Water District in Washington State. Mark had come up the hard way, with hard work and pluck.

Even before he left high school, he restored a sunken eighteen-foot gillnetter and fished out of Bellingham Bay. After a while, he managed to save enough money to buy a $10,000 diesel engine; he wanted the engine because he wanted a bigger boat. He managed to get a loan and

19

built a 36-foot gillnetter he called the *St. Mark*. Other boats followed, including *The Kit*, his first seine boat, in 1976. So did success.

One year, fishing for herring out of San Francisco, he caught $105,000 worth of fish in one week. After expenses, he cleared $95,000 and forged an immutable philosophy. Once, when his sister Laurie fished with him, she had the nerve to complain about the conditions.

"Those fish stink," she told her brother.

"That's the smell of money," he replied.

Ever the entrepreneur, as Mark outgrew one boat, he looked for a new one; he started thinking about replacing *The Kit* as far back as 1981. From the beginning, his watchwords were "diversify" and "maximize." It paid off. He had a custom-built house with a big bar in the kitchen for entertaining guests. Enough cash to put a year's worth of house payments in the bank. Enough spare change to pay all his utility bills.

Mark Coulthurst was a man in a hurry. He told family members that he wanted to retire by the time he was fifty.

That season, starting with the *Investor*, he was taking another leap toward that goal. As one of the newer seine boats, the *Investor* was sleeker, faster, more technologically advanced, more reliable and more versatile. Designed to work multiple, diverse fisheries, it was also much more capital intensive. The most successful skippers—the so-called "highliners" like Mark Coulthurst—hired airborne spotters to locate the vast schools of salmon surging into the mouths of Southeast Alaska's rivers and streams. When the Alaska Department of Fish and Game gave the go-ahead and opened Alaskan waters to commercial fishing, these boats knew where to go and got there quickly. These boats were money machines.

If Mark was always the go-getter, always the hard-charger, his wife Irene represented his softer side. She was, her two sisters-in-law said, "loving, caring and thoughtful." She was the "perfect sister-in-law." She could sew, make stained glass and craft jewelry. She could cook, bake and plan a party for hundreds, and she could run the boat as well as anyone; earlier that very season she had saved the boat from running onto a reef. More than anything, she was proof that Mark Coulthurst didn't make it on his own.

Irene was his high school sweetheart before she was crew, and crew before she was his wife. Together, they were pioneers, always heading toward new horizons. She was there when his career reached a turning point. She knew exactly when it came.

"It happened the first time I went gill-netting with him, when he had the first plywood skiff," she recounted. "The bow was so loaded down with net and fish that I had to sit on top of the outboard motor to keep steerage. Right then I said, 'There's got to be a better way! We've got to have a better plan!' "

As the years went by and their kids were born, Irene found that she really missed being onboard the boat, but couldn't, because daughter Kim and son John were too young. Now that the kids were older, that could change. They planned the *Investor* as a family boat. 1982 was to be the year that the Southeastern salmon season was more than the focal point of Mark's fishing; it was also a time for the family to be together. Togetherness didn't come cheap; the *Investor* was a $750,000 boat with all the modern conveniences.

With his career on the upswing, people in the fishing industry started to notice the young Mr. Coulthurst. So much so, that *Pacific Fishing* magazine wrote a feature story on him for their June 1982 issue. They entitled it, "Mark Coulthurst: Doing the Bellingham Scramble."

The article revealed that Mark bought his newest boat with a loan from the commercial lending division of Seafirst Bank. That took some doing: their accountant was a key player, and Irene dogged their books, as usual. But that's not all the bankers were buying. The Coulthurst's loan officer, Barry Bevis, pointed to Mark Coulthurst. There was something about the man.

"First, Mark is a proven producer," Bevis noted. "Second, he's not trying to grow any faster than his limits allow. Third, he's not afraid of using debt to his advantage, but he's very conscientious about servicing his debt obligation."

"And, I guess one of the things that's obvious about Mark is that he zigs when others zag. But he doesn't do it with his eyes closed. He won't be gambling. He'll be investing."

As proof, when the 1982 season began Mark had the *Investor* ready for almost anything. With three gill-netters in tow, he headed out for Petersburg and Prince William Sound, where his crew tendered roe herring and Mark gillnetted. Coulthurst then teamed up with Dave Harrison of the *Rachel II* for the Togiak herring run, prior to taking the *Investor* to Cordova for a run at Dungeness crab and halibut. Come July, he brought up his family and headed to Southeastern Alaska for the salmon seine season.

That wasn't the only pie he had in the oven. In 1979, at the ripe old age of 23, he formed the Angel Island Pacific Salmon Co., with three partners. The idea was to buy quality seine fish from select vessels and wholesale it worldwide on the fresh market.

"It's not something you try to make a killing with but it's just one more little advantage, that little extra nickel that means another $5,000 at the end of season," Coulthurst told *Pacific Fishing* reporter Doug McNair. "Also, it's brought me much closer to the fishery. I understand it from an entirely different perspective now.

"At the end of five years, I don't want to have to spend 150 days a year on the boat, away from my family," Coulthurst added. "The idea behind the name *Investor* is that we expect the boat to earn money, money that we'll invest in other areas."

As the evening wound down at Ruth Ann's, Mark Coulthurst seemed happy with all he'd wrought—but was he? That night in the restaurant, he argued with someone, possibly over money. One of the waitresses seemed to remember a rude guest who arrived late and got in her way when she tried to clear the Coulthurst's table.

Mark Coulthurst moved on. That was his nature—to go up, over and around obstacles, just as he had after his disastrous first season in Alaska, when their gear and boat proved inadequate. As he and his family returned to the *Investor* that Sunday evening, the young skipper planned to make one more fishing trip with the remaining four crewmembers; as always, the goal was to maximize their return. And then they'd call it quits for the season.

Mark Coulthurst didn't know that this night was his last.

3

The enormity of the crime thrust Alaska's far-flung law enforcement community into action. Trooper Anderson had orders to send the bodies on the first plane out of Craig. On the day after the fire, he arrived at the cannery warehouse at eight o'clock in the morning. By nine, he'd taken the body bags to the seaplane float. By ten, the *Investor* remains were on their way to Ketchikan. At eleven, the first of the big guns began to arrive.

Captain M. C. "Mike" Kolivosky, the commander of the A Detachment of the Alaska State Troopers, arrived from Juneau with his Deputy Commander, Lieutenant Roger McCoy. Kolivosky and McCoy were followed in quick succession by a floatplane bearing Ketchikan prosecuting attorney Mary Anne Henry. Accompanying Henry were two investigators from the Criminal Investigation Bureau in Anchorage: Sergeant Chuck Miller, lead homicide investigator with the team, and Sergeant Jim Stogsdill, an arson investigator.

They had a lot of ground to cover. Prince of Wales Island, where Craig is situated, is 2231 square miles, the third largest island in the United States and slightly larger than Delaware. The place is nothing if not isolated. Located on the western slope of the island, the village faces the Gulf of Alaska. Even at the peak of summer, it is subject to the whims of Pacific storms bringing wind, rain and fog. The nearest population center is Ketchikan, 56 miles and a world away.

This is a land of wall-to-wall forests, crowded with old-growth Sitka spruce, western hemlock and Alaska yellow cedar. A landscape broken only by a sprinkling of bogs and impudent creeks. A place where steep mountains rise abruptly from a sea that laps deep fjords and countless glacial-carved bays.

During the peak fishing season, thousands of fishermen make their way through this village of five hundred full-time residents, stopping briefly for provisions and a side trip to the bars. Surrounding it is a wilderness of small communities with names like Thorne Bay, Whale Pass and Coffman Cove; of Native Alaskan villages like Klawock, home to many Tlingit people, and Kasaan and Hydaburg, home to many Haida people. The only way on or off the island is by boat or plane. The investigators had to check all possible escape routes and, because the fishing season was at its end, they had to work quickly.

After speaking to witnesses, investigators started to gain insight into their chief suspect, a man seen leaving the scene of the crime in the *Investor's* skiff. The crew of the *Casino*, Bruce Anderson and his wife, Jan Kittleson, described a young man in his early twenties, probably wearing "those old kind of black glasses" and a baseball hat. The skiffman handled the skiff expertly, they told troopers, like he knew what he was doing. He seemed to know the local area, because he'd made a point of going around the marker buoy off Crab Bay and avoiding the rocks. Both witnesses emphasized that the skiffman didn't strike them as being a crewmember; they knew Mark Coulthurst and his crew, so that was an important clue.

The *Casino* crew added other crucial details. They insisted that the *Investor* was an "immaculate vessel" that was "unbelievably equipped" and little prone to a fire of the sort they'd witnessed. The skipper added, the fire had taken off quickly, suggesting that an accelerant had been used.

Sue Domenowske and Paul Page were at the cannery dock when the skiffman landed. Sue described a man in his late teens or early twenties, with thin brown hair. She said the man offered her the use of his skiff to go out to the fire, which she thought strange—she didn't know how to operate a power skiff. She said the man spoke slowly, like he wasn't very bright, or was in shock. After their brief conversation, the skiffman went up the dock and disappeared. Domenowske added that he didn't look like anyone she'd ever seen in town. Her boyfriend Paul, described a skiffman remarkably like the one seen by the *Casino* crew—young, blonde, wearing glasses.

Troopers also interviewed Jim Robinson, the owner of Craig Auto, the lone gas station in town. Robinson told them he thought a guy had walked up to get some gas, but he wasn't sure if it was Monday, the day before the fire, or Tuesday. He remembered telling the guy to go ahead and pump his own gas. Said he was a "real decent type." Said he recalled that he was wearing a blue hat, but then said it could have been black. Thought he was "kind of a young guy." Said he might have been wearing glasses.

Beyond those vague descriptions, the gas station owner wasn't sure of anything; he said he got a lot of young guys coming in off boats and asking for gas. Usually they carried jerry jugs, the ubiquitous gasoline containers copied from World War II German designers. Usually it was all right for them to go ahead and pump their own gas.

Frustrated with the gas station owner's lack of clarity about a person who might have been their chief suspect, investigators tracked down yet another witness. Not surprisingly, this young man revealed that his encounter with the *Investor* skiff occurred while he was making his way toward the fire by boat. The skiffman, he revealed, was wearing a baseball-type hat with a seal on the front. He couldn't remember if the suspect had any facial hair and estimated that their boats were between one hundred and two hundred yards away from each other as they passed.

The search for witnesses continued. They found one above the Craig gas station, and he told troopers he had seen a white male adult come in to request gas on the Monday before the fire. He said the man was carrying a red jerry jug, was possibly wearing a halibut jacket and had something on his head—probably a baseball cap.

Not everyone agreed on the skiffman's description, however. Investigators found another witness who claimed to have seen the *Investor* skiff on Tuesday at two o'clock, more than two hours before the fire. The skiff operator, he said, "was a middle-aged native man with medium height and stocky build." The witness didn't pay attention to which direction the skiffman went, didn't see what color of clothes he had on, and didn't know what his facial expressions were.

Then, on the day after the fire, troopers appeared to get a breakthrough. They were combing the village, looking for a man who fit the description of the skiffman seen leaving the fire scene. Local resident Jerry Mackie was there to assist. Just twenty at the time, Mackie was the uniformed local Village Safety Patrol Officer responsible for search and rescue, emergency medical aid and, sometimes, law enforcement.[3] He started his search at the airline terminal on the chance the killer had taken a floatplane out of town. No luck.

His next stop was the Hill Bar. This venerable Craig establishment seemed like a logical place to check, not only because it was just up the road from the airline terminal, but because Mackie's mom was the owner. Mackie slid through the front door and poked his head in far enough to see everyone inside. He saw ten, maybe fifteen people, tops. He scanned the room, trying to make eye contact with each one of them. For the most part, the patrons looked up from their beers, noticed him in his blue trooper coveralls and went back to what they'd been doing.

But one guy was different. This guy turned and, when he saw Mackie walk in, fixed his eyes on him. He looked away, then looked back, then looked away, then looked back again. His nervousness caught Mackie's attention—he thought the guy seemed really shifty and "kind of hinky."

Mackie wasn't sure what was going on, but one thing was certain. This guy had "that look in his eye." The effect was chilling, so chilling that Mackie could hardly describe it. Something told him this was someone the troopers should talk to. "This is the guy," he told himself. "He fits the description."

Mackie remembered the skiffman's description because it so closely matched his own. At five foot ten, the suspect was a little shorter than he was. At 150 pounds, he was a little lighter. He was in his early twenties—the same age as he was—with light brown hair. "This is the guy," he repeated.

From the expansive front windows of the bar, Mackie could see Capt. Kolivosky, Trooper Anderson and another investigator standing in front of J.T. Brown's, a dry goods store that sold sleeping bags, guns and the other essentials of Alaskan life. He scurried down the streets of Craig, which had been torn up to make way for a sewer line, and told

---

3   The Village Public Safety Officer Program began in the late 1970's as a means of providing rural Alaskan communities with needed public safety services at the local level. The program was designed to train and employ individuals residing in the village as first responders to public safety emergencies such as search and rescue, fire protection, emergency medical assistance, crime prevention and basic law enforcement.

them what he'd seen. "There's a man in my mom's bar who matches the guy seen in the *Investor* skiff," Mackie excitedly told them. "And he's acting real nervous."

Kolivosky sent Trooper Anderson scampering back to the city float to roust the crew of the *Casino*. He wanted them to take a look at this guy: The troopers had no time to waste and, of all the witnesses, the *Casino* crew was the only one who could get there quickly; Sue Domenowske and Paul Page, for example, lived on the other side of the island.

By the time they got to the Hill Bar, court records reveal, Bruce Anderson and Jan Kittleson had decided this wasn't going to be a lot of fun. The previous evening, on learning of the murders, they'd slept little. They'd extinguished the diesel stove on their vessel to make sure they could hear people approaching; closed the curtains to hide themselves from prying eyes; locked the windows; put chains across the galley door. All night long, Bruce and Jan worried each other about who and what they'd seen.

Now, at the Hill Bar, the pair was instructed to, "Just amble through" the bar, one at a time, and see if anyone reminded them of the mysterious skiffman. But picking a murderer out of a crowd wasn't something they normally did. They felt apprehensive, scared, even terrified.

Bruce gallantly offered to go first, while Jan waited outside, pretending to talk on the pay phone. As Bruce Anderson passed the small partition that separated the front door from the bar itself, he stopped dead in his tracks. He didn't want to make a spectacle of himself and he didn't want to go any deeper into the bar. Already, the bartender was staring at him. Already, he felt everyone's eyes on him.

But Bruce wasn't sure what he was looking for. He hoped to be struck by an "Aha!" of instant recognition. What he saw was several people sitting at the counter and a few others scattered through the room. He looked them over one-by-one—concentrating on their basic body shape and head—then left as abruptly as he had come. Now it was Jan's turn.

Jan felt uneasy, but unlike her husband, she managed to get past the main entrance of the bar. She walked slowly as she moved between the tables toward the men at the bar. Unlike her husband, she was looking for someone specific—someone wearing old-fashioned black glasses. But Jan was nervous, too, and in less than a minute and a half she had completely traversed the bar. Thirty seconds later, she was back on the street with her husband.

Bruce Anderson told the troopers he had not seen the skiffman. Jan Kittleson told them the same: she hadn't seen anyone that fit the skiff operator's description. Captain Kolivosky decided he wanted to take a look at this guy himself. After all, Mackie had been almost too excited for words when he'd seen the guy. Like Bruce Anderson before him, Kolivosky paused at the end of the partition in the Hill Bar. And like Bruce Anderson, he felt everyone in the room turn their attention toward him. "Which guy were you referring to?" he asked Mackie.

Mackie looked through the bar and noticed that the guy had moved from the middle of the bar to a spot closer to the front windows. He had moved to a spot, in fact, which gave him a better view of downtown Craig. Mackie gestured toward the twentyish-looking man sitting by himself at the bar—the one with the dirty-blonde hair. "The guy" kept looking back at the troopers, just as he had when Mackie entered the bar the first time. And, like before, everyone else quickly returned to their drinks and conversations. "Mackie was right," Kolivosky thought. "There's something about this guy." To Kolivosky's way of thinking, he deserved more attention. The Captain walked into the bar and introduced himself, then asked the young man to step outside.

"I need to see some identification," Kolivosky said as they stood on the gravel path outside the bar.

The Washington State driver's license told Kolivosky this man was John Kenneth Peel. Kolivosky explained why they were questioning him: someone had been seen leaving the *Investor* fire and some people thought he fit the description. John Peel replied that he knew the *Investor* crew; they were friends of his; he had worked for them on Mark Coulthurst's previous boat, *The Kit,* and had fished on that vessel the previous season. His curiosity aroused, Kolivosky asked Peel if he knew anything else. Peel said he had no additional information.

Kolivosky handed back the driver's license and let Mr. Peel go, but he wasn't entirely satisfied. This guy fit the description, twenties, medium length blonde hair, five foot ten, 150 pounds. What was particularly uncanny, as far as Kolivosky was concerned, was the fact that Mackie had picked this guy out of a crowd.

Of all the people Mackie could have picked, this was someone who happened to know the *Investor* crew. This was a guy who happened to have fished with them the previous season. This was a guy who happened to be friends with the victims.

Still, the Captain took a measured approach when he wrote up the encounter in his notes. His entry for September 8th read, cryptically, "1:20. Attempt to locate witnesses. Hill Bar. John Peel. Possible suspect. Negative."

The big question now was, "What next?"

As they headed downtown, Trooper Anderson remembered something. The cold storage employee, the young man who had left for college, had told him there was one other person who'd seen the skiff operator. Maybe, he reasoned, this witness could positively identify John Peel as the man seen fleeing the *Investor*. With precious time already lost to the killer, Kolivosky sent Anderson off to round up the witness. They would meet, they decided, at the old cannery dock, on the other side of town.

While Kolivosky and company waited near the cannery, they saw John Peel heading their way. He walked along Craig's main street, headed down the cannery dock, stopped at a worn-down seine boat named the *Libby No. 8* and started talking to her crew. From what they could tell, he knew them well.

When Anderson brought the witness a short time later, Kolivosky directed him to walk down the dock. The Captain pressed him to take a close look at the people standing at the cannery. "See if any of them match the person operating the *Investor* skiff," he told him.

The heavyset man, known as "Fat Charlie" Clark to his friends, walked to the edge of the dock and cast a steady gaze at the *Libby 8* crew. Then he stepped away from Kolivosky to get a closer view. As he turned to walk back in the Captain's direction, he shook his head to say, "No."

Kolivosky pointed at John Peel, the man who had so recently produced such a strong feeling of suspicion. "Okay, how about that guy?" Kolivosky asked. "Can you identify him as the skiff operator?"

What Captain Kolivosky heard the man say was, "Oh, that's John Peel. No, I know him."[4]

Kolivosky thanked the witness for this trouble and let him go. The suspect that held such promise now appeared to be nothing more than a ghost in the wind.

---

4 Four years later, Clark would change his story and say under oath that he didn't know John Peel in 1982. He added that, while he had seen the *Investor* skiff as he headed to the fire, he wasn't close enough to identify the man at the wheel.

4

Bellingham, Washington
September 10 – 18, 1982

Lisa Coulthurst, Laurie Coulthurst's younger sister, had known John Peel for years. They had dated in high school (not seriously—he was going out with two other girls at the same time) but they did dress up and go out to dinner a few times. He was not her first choice either—especially after he stood her up once—but he was cute, he could be charming and they had fun together. He was popular, although Lisa realized not everybody liked him.

When she thought about it, mostly she remembered them doing "group things." Like ten of them piling into John's gigantic old Lincoln Continental and going inner-tubing down the Nooksack River; like going to keggers, at least one of which was at Lisa's house; like smoking dope together at school or on the weekends.

The two of them had a private joke about smoking dope, one that started in high school. The joke started because, while Lisa smoked dope, she didn't know how to roll joints. She made John Peel do it. "Hey, wanna do me a favor," became a favorite refrain when she needed him to roll a joint. After a while, both of them were saying it, even when no marijuana was involved.

When John went to work for her brother, Mark, in 1980, Lisa could take at least partial credit. She thought of it as a lifesaver because, at the time, John was thinking about going into the military. He was sitting on the Coulthurst's couch when Mark asked him if he'd rather go fishing instead. John said, "yes," and the rest, as they say, is history. She gained a new reason to keep their friendship, although it was complicated by the jealousy of his then-girlfriend, Cathy.

Even after Mark fired him from his boat *The Kit*—before the upgrade to the *Investor*—she still considered him a friend. Enough so that he was the first person she called when she learned Mark's boat had burned in Craig. She knew John had been in Craig and called his parent's house in Bellingham almost immediately.

Lisa talked to John's younger brother, Robert, who said John wasn't back yet but was expected soon. Lisa kept calling for John during the next couple of days—and each time was told John was expected back in Bellingham at any time. At one point she got the feeling that Robert Peel was stalling her or putting her off.

The two of them finally spoke at the end of the week. Lisa was relieved when John Peel said he'd come over and chat. He was good as his word. But when he arrived at the Coulthurst family home near Bellingham, he wasn't alone. He brought Cathy, now his wife. Lisa wasn't alone, either. Though Big John and his wife Sally were still in Ketchikan making arrangements for their deceased family members, Lisa's then-boyfriend (and soon-to-be husband) was there.

When he walked in the door, Lisa noticed that John Peel looked scruffy, which was not surprising considering he'd just gotten back from fishing. He was wearing one of those crummy baseball hats that fishermen wear. The first words out of his mouth were, "Hey, wanna do me a favor?"

After some nervous laughter at John Peel's awkward remark, the four of them sat at the kitchen counter. The day was turning to evening, but the lights at the counter were dim. No one felt comfortable, though everyone no doubt had different reasons. Then again, John didn't really have much to say. "I don't know anything," he told Lisa.

"Did you see any of them before the fire," Lisa asked.

"I saw Kimberly and John and I was giving John a push on a rope swing that they'd made for the boat," Peel replied. Beyond that, Lisa couldn't remember him saying much more. She did notice that he never took his hat off, and she couldn't get over his complexion. He was unshaven, but his face looked like it was scarred or something. His complexion, she thought, was unusually ruddy.

When it came time to leave, Lisa followed John and Cathy Peel through her parent's garage toward the broad, gravel driveway in front of the house. Her boyfriend stayed behind. When they reached the edge of the gravel, John lingered a second, letting his wife get ahead of him. Lisa stayed back with John, who turned and gave her a hug.

He didn't say a thing. Just hugged her briefly and drifted toward his car. Before he got there, he stopped and looked back at Lisa. She thought he was trying to say something but didn't know how. His look said, "I'm sorry," but he didn't say a word.

5

Craig, Alaska
Wednesday, September 8 - Saturday, September 11, 1982

The challenging task of conducting the scene investigation fell to Sgts. Miller and Stogsdill. Sgt. Miller had been a trooper for fifteen years and, like most troopers, had been all over Alaska. A robust-looking man with jet-black hair and a bushy mustache, he had been with the CIB since January of 1973. He'd seen it all: he'd investigated murders by professional hit men, investigated the contract killing of a psychopath by a motorcycle gang in Anchorage and investigated numerous family beefs that had turned bloody.

Sergeant Jim Stogsdill's career had followed a different path. Unlike Miller, his career had only recently focused on criminal investigations. In 1981, when he made sergeant, the troopers decided to make him an arson investigator. After training in Chicago and two weeks of on-the-job training in Washington State, the *Investor* fire was his first major arson investigation. His would be, literally, a baptism by fire.

As soon as they arrived, the two investigators motored out to the *Investor*. They figured they would be spending most of their time there anyway. Already Stogsdill was talking about moving it to a dry dock. Then he could begin the debrisment—the laborious process of sifting through the ashes for whatever clues remained. Trooper Anderson struck a cautionary note. Not only had the boat burned, but it was full of water from various, sometimes unsuccessful, attempts to put out the fire.

"I don't think we're going to be able to move it to dry dock," he told Stogsdill, "but you can judge that for yourself."

At the scene, the troopers found the *Investor* still smoldering. After grabbing buckets of seawater to beat down the flames, and a brief survey of the boat, Miller and Stogsdill reached a conclusion: if they moved the *Investor*, she would probably sink and they'd lose valuable evidence. Besides, as Trooper Anderson pointed out, Craig didn't even have a grid large enough to accommodate a boat of that size—much less a dry dock.[5]

The scene investigation would take place where the *Investor* lay, hard on the shore of Fish Egg Island, subject to the fluctuations of the tide, exposed to the wind and weather, heeled over and listing when there was enough water to keep her afloat. But before the debrisment could begin, there was housekeeping to be done. Sensing that the *Investor's* anchor winch was going to be in their way, the troopers called in a logging helicopter and had it removed.

With the anchor winch off the bow and on the beach, the troopers began to check off the other things they'd need. Some sort of float, tied up alongside the *Investor*, would stabilize the vessel as well as provide a platform for the debrisment. Shovels and screens were needed to sift through the charred structure for evidence. And they needed something to store evidence.

Immediately, the large plastic totes used to store fish came to mind, if only because they promised to be readily available. That evening, at the Craig police department, Stogsdill and Miller made arrangements for everything they'd need. The Craig police chief wouldn't let them go before telling them he feared the fire on the *Investor* would flare up again and burn all their evidence. Stogsdill agreed but wanted to know what the police chief could do to help.

"We've got some foam we could use," the chief gamely offered, still stinging from an earlier rebuff when the "big boys" had turned him away. Stogsdill took him up on his offer. Later that evening, in a matter of five minutes, the chief extinguished the *Investor* fire once and for all.

Miller and Stogsdill spent two and a half days on the *Investor*. The crime scene was far from ideal. The still-smoldering vessel had been

---

5   A grid is an arrangement of vertical and horizontal pilings, which serve as a makeshift dry dock. Boats tie up to the vertical pilings when the tide is in and drop down onto the horizontal pilings as the tide goes out. At low tide, the boat is completely out of the water; painting and other repairs can then be performed until the next tide comes in.

severely deformed by the fire; the port side of the hull had collapsed near the bow; the foredeck, from amidships to the exhaust stack, had fallen in and been compromised by the heat. The engine room and fish hold, meanwhile, were awash in hundreds of gallons of water. The boat was keeled over and, when the tide came in, wave after wave lapped across her deck, scattering whatever happened to be in its path. The deck itself was slick and dangerous—and the weather only made it worse.

September turns to rain in southeast Alaska and these days were no exception. The clouds sprawled low, clutching the deep green forests that clotted the islands. The sky turned into a spreading lump of mottled gray. Bone-numbing downpours snuck through in clusters, breaking only to catch their breath.

The debrisment began unceremoniously, with Miller and Stogsdill first removing the larger pieces of debris that obscured the deck. Beneath that layer, they found that the actual structure of the vessel—fiberglass, with the resin burned out of it—had folded in or broken off into chunks. Only by peeling back or discarding that two or three-foot layer of overburden could they get at the smaller debris that rested below. Each time they spied something suspicious, they photographed it in place and put it in an evidence bag. When they finished that, it was time for another shovelful. When the fish tote was completely full, it weighed forty or fifty pounds—and then it was time to move it down to the float for additional sifting.

The sifting process was no less laborious. Here, at least, they had help. The Craig police chief started by shoveling a load onto shrimp screens perched atop garbage cans. Then Trooper Anderson shook and shuffled the debris across the quarter-inch wire mesh, looking for anything Miller or Stogsdill might have missed. The work was mindless but unpleasant. The contents of the fish tubs were mostly a foul-smelling, deep-black slurry. And only when they'd determined that the contents were of no significance could they shovel it over the side.

While Miller dug through the still-steaming debris, Stogsdill intermittently swept the area with a "sniffer" designed to detect gasoline and other hydrocarbons. Stogsdill hoped he would find hidden evidence of accelerants used by the arsonist. The first significant find wasn't an accelerant, but a rifle in the remains of a storage locker snug in the bow of the boat. The weapon showed the ravages of fire and the efforts to put it out. The wooden stock was missing. The metallic parts were rusted. Miller immediately recognized it as a Ruger Mini-14 semi-automatic rifle. Nearby, in the crew quarters, they spotted a fire extinguisher buried in the rubble, with only its top protruding. The activation pin hadn't been pulled; no one on board had even attempted to use it.

As the first day progressed, Miller and Stogsdill went down on their hands and knees, and sorted through the debris by hand. Soon, they found bones and bone fragments. They carefully plucked them out of the ashes. Everything else in the vicinity, including what looked like burned chunks of human tissue, was taken over to the screens and sifted again.

At midday of the first day, Miller found another body. Located on the upper starboard side of the crew quarters, it had been substantially burned by the fire. It was recognizably human, even though there was not much left beyond the chest wall and a few ribs. Nearby, they found additional remains: an arm that had presumably become detached from the body during the fire.

As they moved across the centerline of the crew quarters, to an area on the port side of the vessel, they found additional bones; some were recognizable as pieces of rib or vertebrae. They also found a few metal fragments. Despite their early finds, however, Miller and Stogsdill shoveled and scraped for the rest of the first day without discovering anything else of importance. Their only reward was a healthy supply of aches and pains—and a firsthand view of a seemingly endless store of destruction.

On the second day, they reached the engine room of the *Investor*. The boat's structure was so compromised that Miller and Stogsdill had to squat. Their only consolation was that they weren't alone; hovering nearby were two representatives from Delta Marine, the company that built the *Investor*.

In the engine room, the four men found by-products of the fire everywhere. The battery case had exploded, leaving behind an acid residue; the hydraulic tank had ruptured, adding a petroleum stain to the engine room environment. Smoke and soot from the fire had permeated the space. Here and there, the troopers spotted a black goo that coated pipes and other exposed equipment. The halon fire-suppression system had gone off, bringing its own contribution to the atmosphere inside that room.

What they didn't find, however, were additional bodies or signs of human remains. They also reached the conclusion that the fire had not started there. Other than the obvious effects of the combustibles, the engine room was fairly clean: only one side had been exposed to fire.

When the boat builders examined the engine room more closely, however, they noticed something unusual: all of the butterfly valves for the boat's pumping system had been opened. Normally, that system was used to bring in brine for refrigerating the fish hold and was used only when there were fish in the hold. To purposefully bring water into an empty fish hold risked a potentially dangerous situation, particularly when the vessel was underway. So dangerous that only the skipper and his chief engineer were allowed to open those valves. Rarely, if ever, were all the valves left in that position. The experts from Delta Marine could only reach one conclusion: someone had tried to sink the *Investor*.

As the second day reached its end, the troopers returned to the main deck and the galley. They intended to work their way back to the main bulkhead that separated the fore part of the boat from the fish hold, then quit for the day. But the search turned up more evidence of human remains—part of a foot and a few other bone fragments; they also found two lower leg bones and a plain gold band that appeared to be a wedding ring. Now, the search would continue until they lost daylight.

On moving the search into the surrounding area, court records indicate that they found additional body parts. These remains consisted of nothing more than a few tiny fragments of bone. Still, they were carefully placed in a separate bag and marked. Like everything they'd found before this, these remains were headed for Anchorage where they would be examined by the coroner.

On Saturday, the troopers made their final discovery. On the aft of the *Investor* was a fancy hydraulic ramp for moving her power skiff in and out of the water. On close inspection, it was apparent the skiff ramp had been damaged. This was not fire related: there was very little evidence of any heat damage to this part of the vessel.

The best the troopers could figure was that someone had tried to remove the skiff, but didn't know how to operate the ramp. Someone had used the boat's hydraulic system and forced the skiff off the *Investor*. Whether the product of inexperience, haste or panic, the troopers thought it meaningful.

With the search of the vessel's decks and interior finally at an end, Sergeant Miller decided there was only one more place to examine: the *Investor's* exterior. Sometimes wading in waist-deep water, Miller slowly made his way toward the stern. He ultimately got as far back as her propeller. He was looking for any hidden damage, any signs of violence to the hull, any indications that there had been a struggle at Ben's Cove. What Miller found was some damage in the bow, apparently caused by the firefighters when they pushed her onto the beach. Other than that, the *Investor* was free of harm, except for what looked like the scrapes and scuffs of normal operation.

When Miller finished with the *Investor's* exterior, it was 5:30 in the evening on Saturday, September 11th. They were done for the day, and they were done with the debrisment. They had examined the *Investor* from stem to stern. They had found everything they were going to find.

Based on their scene investigation, they knew someone had tried to sink the *Investor*. That someone had also broken the pins on the skiff ramp at the back of the boat. This perpetrator was in such a hurry to get out of there, he just cranked up the hydraulics and forced the skiff off the back of the boat. Stogsdill, meanwhile, was fairly certain the fire was arson. Miller thought he knew why the boat was torched. After failing to sink the boat, the killer found himself in a shocking position come Tuesday.

"This person is thinking 'oh shit,' " Miller speculated. 'She's still visible. I better go back. People have seen me—or I think people have seen me. I better burn that boat.' This individual is associated with the crime scene and he wants to destroy it."

But Miller's speculation didn't get much further than that. The on-shore investigation had been a disappointment. Worse yet, it had been less than methodical. They had a description of the suspect, but no suspect. They had a half-dozen witnesses, but no composite drawings of the skiffman. The closest they had come to a possible suspect was a former Coulthurst crewman—and none of the witnesses were able to identify him. According to Kolivosky, one witness even said he knew the guy and that the former Coulthurst crewman was not the person he'd seen in the *Investor's* skiff.

Townspeople in Craig, meanwhile, had gotten very nervous. Rumors were flying in every direction. People who'd never done so before were now locking their doors. What troopers needed more than anything, Miller knew, was a quick arrest. Then, maybe the people in Craig would be more willing to talk. But as far as anyone could tell, an arrest was still over the horizon.

Miller and Stogsdill resolved to push harder.

LATER THAT MONTH THEY RETURNED to Craig where, under the guidance of arson investigator Barker Davie, they reexamined the *Investor* for signs of arson. As they surveyed the stern, and then the galley, Davie pointed out what seemed to be two fires of separate and distinct intensities. One was at the back of the vessel, near the seine net; the other was in the general area of the galley and crew quarters, toward the bow of the boat.

Davie told the troopers that the extensive damage in the forward part of the boat strongly suggested that gasoline or some other fuel had been used to accelerate the fire. Given the size of the boat and the amount of damage that stretched before him, the arson expert estimated that anywhere from two and a half to five gallons of highly flammable material had been dumped on the *Investor* and set aflame.

That's not all their investigation revealed. After examining what seemed like miles of wire at an abandoned Klawock fish cannery just north of Craig that Trooper Anderson had commandeered, they discovered no evidence of an electrical fire. They left Klawock with an ever-stronger feeling the *Investor* was torched by an arsonist trying to cover up a crime.

6

Bellingham, Washington
Saturday, September 18, 1982

B ellingham is the northernmost major city in Washington State, only 23 miles from the Canadian border. Bounded by the Cascade Mountains on the east and Puget Sound on the west, her early history was defined by the twin engines of lumber and fishing. By the 1980s, those economic engines had declined. Lumber faded. Fishing plummeted. Overfishing, and court decisions that gave a larger share of the catch to the Washington tribes, sent many of the non-native fishermen north.

When fishing fell, Bellingham's identity shifted. The single largest presence in the city was Western Washington State University. More than anything, Bellingham had become a college town. Yet it wasn't entirely so. The university, for all its influence, seemed to spin in a separate orbit. When Bellingham went to work, it drove to the pulp mill, to the aluminum plant, to the oil refineries. When Bellingham went to play, it went to the mountains, to the streams, to the sea. There was something oddly schizophrenic about the place, but the Coulthursts' funeral brought everyone together.

The crowd outside St. Paul's Episcopal church stretched toward Eldridge Street, their backs to Bellingham Bay and the boat harbor. Some stood on the historic church's front steps. A few were able to peek into the church through the open door, which cast a narrow shaft of light past the baptismal font at the rear of the sanctuary. Inside the brick-walled church, the pews were crowded. So were the aisles. The dark wood of the church's vaulted ceiling seemed to match the somber mood of the crowd. Always a risky pursuit, the dangers of commercial fishing held their souls in common bond. But murder was a leap beyond what anyone expected; fishermen from up and down the West Coast had come to pay their last respects.

Nearly eight years had passed since these friends last gathered at St. Paul's. That occasion was a happier one: Mark Coulthurst's marriage to Irene Hudson. They were in their early twenties then. They picked the same church where John and Sally Coulthurst got married, thirty years before. The only thing that hadn't changed was the neighborhood.

This area of fine mansions, many of them from the turn of the century, was still proud of its past. Many of the homes had brass placards announcing when they had been built and who originally lived there. Most of their present owners had restored them to their past glory. Just being here brought back memories for the Coulthurst family.

They remembered that this church was crammed with three hundred guests for Mark and Irene's wedding. They remembered that at eleven o'clock on the wedding night, over a hundred people were still celebrating at the Coulthurst house. Irene, they remembered, was in her dirty blue jeans, dressed for a honeymoon trip to the Oregon coast. They recalled, too, how Mark had packed their truck with a camp stove, lanterns, sleeping bags, tarps and groceries, and how Mark had surprised Irene and instead taken her to Hawaii.

"He had to buy her new clothes when they got there," Sally Coulthurst recalled. "Because she didn't have a damn thing to wear when she got to Hawaii."

The family remembered, too, that Mark and Irene were high school sweethearts. That they had broken up just before the prom, when Mark started going out with the only other girl he'd ever dated. Shortly after that, he'd thrown out his shoulder doing wheelies on his motorcycle. Both girls showed up at the hospital to see him; by the time he left the hospital, Irene was his girl, again.

Now, as organ music wafted through the church, their eyes were drawn to the chancel. Off to the side were two memorials to the *Investor's* dead crew: a red-and-white rose ship's wheel and a yellow rose anchor. To bring this chapter full circle, the same minister who married them would perform the eulogy.

"Eight years ago I was officiating at a wedding right here," the Reverend W. Robert Webb said as he began addressing the mourners. "But I didn't have the papers. Since I had arrived at the last minute, I was hurrying to complete them."

"We got through the, 'Mark do you,' and 'Irene do you' parts," he continued. "But when I got to the blessing, I didn't use 'Irene Hudson.' I used 'Laurie Hudson,' her maid of honor. As I was finishing, Irene whispered to me, 'I don't want Mark to marry my sister!' "

"He didn't," Webb intoned, his voice solemn and serious. "And now Irene will be married to Mark for eternity."

As the throng trickled out after the memorial service, Sergeants Miller and Stogsdill mingled among them. It was a chance to get a good look at the crowd; perhaps there was a killer in their midst. Seeing nothing unusual, they moved on.

After the memorial, the troopers went to the short list of people they wanted to see. Not coincidentally, these folks had all worked on the *Libby 8* and were in Craig around the time of the murders. Dawn Holmstrom was on the list because of reported contacts with *Investor* crew members the night before the murders. Larry Demmert was on the list because he was the skipper of the *Libby 8*. John Peel was on the list because he knew the Coulthursts and the *Investor* crew. Of the three, only John Peel seemed to be around.

John Peel met them at the Holiday Inn in Bellingham. He wasn't alone; he'd brought his wife, Cathy. Although Sergeant Miller wasn't expecting her, he didn't send her away. All they wanted, after all, was information about the Coulthursts and the *Investor* crew. When they settled into the hotel room, however, Miller noticed that Cathy Peel seemed nervous.

The interview began with the usual questions, name, date of birth, Social Security number, phone, address, vital statistics. Peel told Miller that he was five feet, ten inches tall. He weighed 150 pounds, and that he was presently unemployed.

Miller wanted to know what John Peel could tell them about the *Investor* crew and their activities on Sunday, September 5th. Peel wasn't much help. He told Miller he was tired on Sunday. That he "crashed" at 6:00 p.m. in the crew quarters of the *Libby 8*. He slept all night and got up the next morning.

When the subject turned to the crew of the *Investor*, Peel had more to say. He had worked with most of them on Mark Coulthurst's previous boat, *The Kit*; he had met other crew members during the 1982 season, while he was on the *Libby 8* and they were on the *Investor*. Contrary to the impression that the *Investor* crew was a bunch of party animals, Peel said, Mike Stewart and Chris Heyman were weight lifters who were into taking vitamins.

Because some of those *Investor* crewmembers were suspects, Miller asked if Mark Coulthurst allowed guns on board, and if he did, who had them. Peel told him that, while they were on *The Kit*, Dean Moon had purchased a rifle. He thought it was "a .22 or something like that." Peel himself said he had purchased a .30-30 rifle. He said that he and Dean purchased these rifles at the same time—1981—and at the same place: J.T. Brown's in Craig. With the interview nearly at an end, Miller gave John Peel his card and told him to call if he had any further information.

As John Peel and his wife left the room, Sergeant Miller couldn't help but feel that something was amiss. Peel hadn't said anything that made him suspicious. That wasn't the problem. The problem was Cathy Peel. Why had he brought her with him? Why was it so important for her to be there during the interview? Did he need moral support? Then there was her behavior during the interview. Cathy Peel had become more nervous as they talked. Miller noticed that, by the end of the interview, she was wringing her hands almost uncontrollably.

Miller pushed it aside. John Peel wasn't a suspect. Kolivosky had cleared him.

7

As September progressed, investigators learned several things. Each one brought them closer to solving the mystery of the fire and the murders. They learned that the skipper, Mark Coulthurst, was on board the *Investor* with his wife and two children. That four additional people had been part of the *Investor* crew: Dean Moon, nineteen; Michael Stewart, nineteen; Chris Heyman, eighteen; and Jerome Keown, nineteen. The first four bodies they'd recovered were x-rayed in Ketchikan. The examination revealed the presence of metal objects, possibly molten metal, possibly bullets.

The coroner quickly identified three bodies: Mark Coulthurst, his wife Irene and their daughter Kimberly. Mark and Irene had been shot several times, each with at least one shot to the head. The other victims were also believed to have been shot, but not enough remained of them to be sure. Troopers knew this much, though: lots of gunshots were fired in the forward cabin, where the bodies were found.

By matching x-rays his family had sent north, a radiologist soon identified the remains of crewmember Michael Stewart, Mark Coulthurst's cousin on his mother's side. They had now positively identified four of the eight people thought to have been aboard the *Investor*. There was still hope they would identify more. They did.

By mid-month, Jerome Keown had been tentatively identified. His body was found on the stairs leading up to the galley of the *Investor*. He had been shot at least once, in the arm. Troopers considered that a defensive injury, one he had suffered while holding his arm up to protect himself from the killer's weapon.

LeRoy Flammang, who left the *Investor* only a week and a half before the murders, told troopers where everyone slept on board the vessel. Kimberly and Irene Coulthurst usually shared one of the two bunks in the stateroom. Johnny Coulthurst, he told them, usually slept in the day bed off the wheelhouse; sometimes he shared a stateroom bunk with his dad. The information about Johnny Coulthurst was particularly telling. The wheelhouse, they knew, was hit the hardest by the fire; it was conceivable that, if Johnny had been sleeping there, his body could have been totally consumed by the fire.

The rest of the crew, Flammang reported, slept in the fo'c's'le—the narrow area located in the bow of the boat. Dean Moon, he told them, had been using the bottom bunk on the starboard side. Mike Stewart had slept in the bunk above him—and his body had in fact been found on the starboard side. Chris Heyman, Flammang said, was on the port side—a place where they had found bones, a watchband and a molar tooth. Flammang himself had slept in the middle bunk, but wasn't sure what the sleeping arrangements were after he'd left. Even at that, the troopers felt a little closer to matching the bodies they had found with the bunks where Flammang thought they had been sleeping.

By month's end, only three bodies remained unidentified. Little Johnny Coulthurst—who at four years old was an unlikely killer, and two crew members, Chris Heyman and Dean Moon.

Based on the coroner's autopsy results, the troopers knew the Coulthursts were dead before the fire started. None of the victims had carbon monoxide in their lungs, which would have been present had they been alive beforehand. Judging from the blood alcohol tests they'd conducted, most of the victims were drunk when they were killed. The pathologist estimated, moreover, that they had only seven bodies. Within weeks, even that changed; the pathologist eventually thought only six bodies had been found on board the *Investor*. The conclusion was obvious. At least one of the *Investor's* eight crewmembers was unaccounted for—and quite possibly a murderer.

Investigators also learned some of the particulars of the crime. They knew that 144 fishing boats had been anchored in and around Craig during the weekend of the murders. They also learned that the *Investor* was rafted up next to two other boats, the *Defiant* and the *Decade*, on the northernmost finger float at North Cove. She docked on Sunday, September 5th.

Early on that Sunday night, witnesses saw Dean Moon and Jerome

Keown head toward town together. The rest of the crew followed shortly thereafter. In town, Moon and Keown soon ran into Dawn Holmstrom from the *Libby 8,* a so-called "cannery boat" crewed by some of their Bellingham friends (including John Peel). They told her that Irene and the children planned to fly back to Washington the following day. Holmstrom told troopers that the three of them made plans to meet up the following day at a local bar. Moon and Keown never showed up.

Back at the North Cove dock, parties were under way on the two boats rafted up to the *Investor.* There was lots of drinking. As far as anyone knew, the *Investor* was empty.

Stogsdill and Miller travelled to Petersburg, Alaska, to find witnesses from the boats rafted up next to the *Investor.* They found three of them. In Sgt. Miller's retelling, Dale Rose of the *Decade,* "weaves out on deck to throw up. From the haze of his illness, he looks up and sees the *Investor* drifting out. He sees a guy in the wheelhouse. He waves. The guy waves back. Rose does his business and goes back inside."

The other fishermen told similar stories. It was the end of the season. They were intoxicated. Each of them awakened early the next morning, sick or hung-over or both. They saw a solitary figure on the *Investor* as it drifted away from the dock and then took off under its own power. None could describe whom they'd seen.

The troopers now strongly suspected that the *Investor* crew was dead before she left Craig.

Things turned more serious when one of them handed over the *Investor's* tie lines, which had been left behind on his boat. That in itself could be taken as evidence of someone trying to conceal a crime. Those tie lines would ultimately be sent to the FBI for fingerprinting.

Then came an interesting detail. On the Monday afternoon after the fire, at 1:30 p.m., a witness recalled, he had spotted the *Investor* skiff tied up at the cold storage dock. The troopers soon learned that Dawn Holmstrom had also seen the skiff, at 8:00 a.m., that same Monday.

Now they had multiple witnesses who'd seen the *Investor's* skiff—in Craig—before the fire. That meant that the killer had returned to town *before* the arson. That meant he had to have gone back to the *Investor* to torch her and then return to town once more. Given that scenario, the chances were high that even more people had seen him. This guy had been in a panic and then in a panic all over again. Surely he'd made some mistakes. Surely those mistakes would come back to haunt him.

Equally revealing: all attempts to contact the *Investor* that day, and inform her skipper about the tie lines, had failed. In addition, investigators learned that, despite the bad weather, several boats had noticed the *Investor* anchored out in Ben's Cove all day Monday. Nobody had seen any activity on board the vessel from the time it left the dock until the time it caught on fire. When that information was combined with the knowledge that the Coulthursts were seen alive at Ruth Ann's restaurant on the evening of Sunday, September 5th, the troopers reached a conclusion. The murders had probably occurred either late Sunday evening or early Monday morning.

As for motives, robbery seemed unlikely, if only because the *Investor* was the third boat out and a robber would have to climb over two other boats just to get there and back. Mark Coulthurst's father had been adamant that his son did not carry cash and had not received a big cash settlement from one of the canneries. Indeed, interviews with the Petersburg fishermen confirmed that on the Sunday night before the murders, Mark Coulthurst had asked one of them to give him $100 in exchange for a check. The man had generously complied because, he said, he trusted Mark Coulthurst.

Additional inquiries determined that the *Investor* probably had not received a large cash settlement before the killings. Fish buyers told them that even the so-called "cash" buyers paid with checks. Equally important, former crewmember LeRoy Flammang kept detailed records of every dime they'd spent during that summer—and every fish they'd sold. They'd sold plenty of fish but Flammang confirmed that Mark Coulthurst rarely kept cash on the *Investor*.

The evidence didn't point to an execution. Mark and Irene were found collapsed upon each other in the galley. Everyone else was found in or near their bunks. More than anything, this seemed like a crime of anger, surprise and fear. Anyone who felt like he had to kill the kids along with the crew probably feared being identified by people he knew. No, a stranger had not murdered these people.

Rumors in Craig pointed to a possible drug connection, so it was a question that had to be asked and answered. Former crewman LeRoy Flammang recalled a young Alaska Native who worked on *The Kit* and sold drugs, mostly marijuana, in big enough quantities for people to take notice. One of the reasons Mark wanted LeRoy to work on the *Investor*, Flammang revealed, was because he was a retired Customs Officer; Mark wanted to give the signal that the *Investor* was not a drug boat. Another former crewman, Roy Tussing, agreed; he said they'd gone through a period when they used them, but that was over with. Work, he said, "was first before anything else." Tussing felt sure that drugs weren't involved in the *Investor* murders. "It got to be that pot wasn't allowed on the boat, you know. Especially while working."

Flammang provided additional insights. When troopers asked him whether there a particular reason he left the boat in late August, the crewman said, "There was not a particular reason. I was tired, you know. We fished, I'm getting up in years and there was an irritation on board. For me, the family and the kids. I'm not used to having little kids under foot anymore."

An irritation caused by having kids on board the boat. An irritation caused by having Mark's wife there too. There were signs of deeper issues. Roy Tussing, who left the boat only days before the murders, spoke of a heated argument with Mark Coulthurst. He told troopers they'd argued over a chronic hydraulic leak that wasn't as easy to fix as the skipper expected. Roy felt Mark was being unreasonable and Mark returned the feeling, saying, "Well, I've kind of had it with you." Feelings on the boat, Tussing added, had gotten pretty low.

"Then after we calmed down, I come back to the boat and we were talking and the guys were up scrubbing, you know, on the boat and stuff," Tussing revealed. "And I said, 'Hey, nobody's happy on this boat.' I go, 'Look it.' I go, 'You don't see a smile or anything like that.' And I go, you know, the guys had a half a day off where they could have… you know, they had to go fishing again right away and they should have been enjoying themselves or, you know, buying an ice cream cone or do[ing] something. And they were up scrubbing the stupid black stuff off the top of the [wheel] house.' "

That's not all the investigators learned. The two former crewmen said Mark Coulthurst was a guy who was full of himself, even cocky. A guy who could be quite aggressive. A guy who, though prone to forgive and forget, did not always suffer fools gladly.

If there was one incident that stuck out in Tussing's mind, it was one he remembered from the bars in Ketchikan some years back. Roy was deep in conversation with another guy at the bar, when Mark walked in, full of himself and full of drink. He immediately picked up on the topic of conversation, and started forcefully offering his opinions. Mark didn't realize it, but Roy saw that his skipper was "really pissing this guy off. He was a lot more sober than Mark. He could've cleaned his clock."

Realizing this, Roy eased Mark away from the guy. He'd averted a potentially dangerous situation. Roy wondered: if he had been on the boat, would he have been able to rescue Mark from one more scrape? This time, he decided, he didn't think so.

8

By the time the *Investor* reached Craig on its final journey, its crew had been fishing for 54 days. According to LeRoy Flammang's log, which recorded when they fished and how much they caught, they started fishing on the Fourth of July. Looking back from September, it seemed like there were two separate and distinct fishing seasons.

The first season was more closures than openers. They fished two days, had four days off in Craig, fished two days, had four days off in Ketchikan, fished two days, had another four days off in Ketchikan, lost one day with a steering problem, fished one day and then had another four days off in Ketchikan. They caught a total of 5,417 fish.

The second season was another matter entirely. For 31 days, they fished almost non-stop. They fished two days at a time to start, but this time there was only one day between openings and that was spent cruising the fishing grounds, scoping for fish. By mid-August, the state of Alaska Department of Fish and Game had turned up the heat on the season. The *Investor* fished four days in a row, took a day off to cruise the fishing grounds, then fished another three days in a row. They fished an estimated six of the next nine days—estimated because LeRoy Flammang had left the boat by then and taken his fish log with him. By the time LeRoy Flammang left, they had caught another 106,815 fish.

When the *Investor* crew reached Craig, they were near the end of a long season. They had worked hard. They wanted to play hard. But deep down, they were almost at the end of their human resources. 21 of the last 31 days had been fishing days. None of them had slept, really. When they were fishing, there was little rest. When they fished, they fished for twelve hours straight.

When they weren't fishing, there was wheel watch. Each of the crewmen took their turn, usually in pairs because it was safer that way. No one escaped having his sleep interrupted for at least two hours every night while the boat was running. They learned to sleep with the dull drone of the engine surrounding them. They learned to sleep without really sleeping.

Meals during this time were taken when they could. While the crew was lucky to have Irene as their cook, for most of the day they could eat only during the twenty-minute period when the net was out. The rest of the time they were either setting the net or hauling it in. Lunch was taken on the run. The skiffman usually ate lunch in the skiff.

Even dinner could become a haphazard affair. Fishing never closed before six in the evening and often went as late as eight. Dinner was always after the last set, no matter when the last set occurred. Sometimes, they were still eating at eight or nine in the evening.

And the next day? The next day always came early. The worst was when they were unloading fish to a tender and most of the crew had to pitch fish. Sometimes it was the middle of the night.

On the Sunday night when they hit Craig, the *Investor* crew likely felt they could finally relax a little bit. Sunday they had off and Monday was a holiday. They wouldn't fish again until Tuesday and when that was done they were finished for the season. But when they hit port, they were tired. When the murderer came on board, they were too tired to fight back. Too tired, or too drunk, or too stoned.

That wasn't the only problem. Though a large, luxurious boat, there was only one way off the *Investor*: through the galley. A killer standing in the galley with a gun could easily block that exit. Unless someone was smart enough to remember the hatch in the fo'c's'le, everyone was trapped; even remembering the hatch might not have been enough, because it took an awkward climb up the bunks to get there. Roy Tussing remembered fighting a losing battle to keep that hatch ajar—crewmembers had a habit of removing the small can be had used to prop it open. With the hatch closed, there was nowhere to go. The killer could shoot his victims at will, and probably did.

9

August 1983 – November 1983

In the year that followed the murders, Sgt. Chuck Miller led an investigation that fielded close to a thousand calls, investigated hundreds of leads and taped nearly as many interviews. They had been up and down the Alaska panhandle, dragged themselves to Washington State enough times to qualify for frequent flyer miles, and even taken a side trip to Indiana.[6] For all that, they were no closer to an arrest than they'd been on day one. During that time, they had gathered as many as a dozen suspects. That was twelve too many.

Then, in August of 1983, Sergeant Miller was transferred out of homicide and into statewide narcotics. His replacement was Sergeant Stogsdill, whose career had bounced him from arson to statewide narcotics and now into homicide. Before Miller handed over the reins on the *Investor* case he held a meeting; he called in the twenty or so troopers from the Criminal Investigation Bureau; he called in Sergeant Roy Holland from the Alaska State Trooper's (AST) Seattle office and

---

6   The Indiana trip was particularly aggravating: a witness seemed to have inside knowledge of the crime, so troopers had to take him seriously. The investigation hinged on their interview of the man who went by the name of T. Rex Mullins. Mullins claimed he personally drove Chris Heyman and Johnny Coulthurst out of Alaska, travelling from Nome to Washington State—a distance of nearly two thousand miles—in a period of 24 hours. That was impossible. After the local police busted him for filing a false report, Mr. Mullins told officers that, if they were interested in finding additional evidence, they should look underneath the cushion in his sofa. What Stogsdill found under the cushion was a magazine called *Detective Cases*. In it, he found an article entitled, "Mystery of the Sailing Skeletons." Everything T. Rex Mullins told them had come from that article. And so it was that a seemingly innocuous article had perpetrated a mean-spirited hoax.

Detective Dave McNeill from the Bellingham Police Department. He asked for help.

Miller believed they had followed every lead they could; he also knew they ended up running off every which way. Maybe they had missed something. Maybe they had taken a wrong turn somewhere. More than anything, though, they had lost focus; they needed, as Miller put it, "to look at this case again real hard."

It was left to Sergeant Stogsdill to take up Miller's challenge. He gathered every case interview and report he could find; after imposing a rough order on the records, he read—and reread—as much as he could. And then, as August drifted toward September, he too held a meeting.

They came to Ketchikan. They came from all over. Sergeants Stogsdill and Flothe, and Trooper Bullington, from Anchorage. Sergeant Israelson from Petersburg. Trooper Anderson from Klawock. Sergeant Demmert, one of Larry Demmert's many relatives, from Fish and Wildlife in Southeast Alaska. Sergeant Holland from Seattle. Sergeant Glass from Ketchikan. In what became known as the "Anniversary Meeting," they did precisely what Miller suggested.

They began by drawing a grid on a blackboard. Sgt. Glenn Flothe, the one cop who could pass as a college professor, took the lead. They started by describing their suspect. The eyewitnesses had provided a physical description, so that went on the grid. They also had a rough idea of the clothing worn by the skiffman; that too went on the grid. Although it seemed obvious, the troopers added "in Craig at the time of the murders."

At the top of their list, however, were two other items. The first of these was "experienced fisherman." Although they knew that all the gauges and controls on the *Investor* were clearly marked, it seemed clear the perpetrator knew more than a little about fishing boats.

The killer had known, for instance, how to move the *Investor* from its moorings and take it to a remote spot off Fish Egg Island. He had known—or thought he had known—how to sink it by opening all the valves in the engine room. He had known—or thought he had known—how to remove the skiff from the stern of the boat. Witnesses who'd seen him operating the *Investor's* skiff described him in glowing terms. This guy knew what he was doing. He had even performed a flawless "power landing," which could hardly be expected of a rank amateur.[7]

When they thought about it, moreover, that wasn't the only demonstration of fishing experience. They remembered that on the day of the fire, as he returned to Craig, that he went around the navigation can that marked the channel—even though it meant traveling a greater distance. Their chief suspect knew enough about local waters to realize what route to take if he wanted to avoid running aground.

The second critical item on the list was "knew the Coulthursts and the *Investor* crew." The vehemence with which both Mark and Irene Coulthurst were shot was revealing; whoever committed these crimes wanted to make sure the primary victims were dead, but then the killer had gone on to kill people beyond his primary victims. Why do that unless they knew him? He had also killed the two Coulthurst children. Why do *that* unless they knew him? Every extra second he spent on board the *Investor* increased his chances of being caught.

The troopers started a separate list for suspects. They had pared their list down to five young men, which was in itself a step in the right direction. By the time they moved their investigation forward, only two of those suspects still mattered. Of the others, two proved to be somewhere other than Craig at the time of the murders. The third, missing crewman Chris Heyman, was a recent high school graduate. He'd spent most of his life in New York City, where he lived with his mother; it was his father in California who got him onto the *Investor*. Chris Heyman was an inexperienced kid; he was streetwise, not boat wise.

Of the remaining suspects, the first was Dean Moon, another *Investor* crewmember whose remains had not been identified. Was he missing and presumed dead, or just missing? As the investigation fanned out from the Anniversary Meeting, the troopers checked off his particulars against their list criteria.

Did Dean Moon match the physical description of the suspect? At least some of the witnesses, shown photos, said he resembled the skiff operator. Though his physical description differed somewhat from that provided by the witnesses—Dean's hair was dark and curly, not blonde

---

7   A "power landing" is one in which the vessel closes in on the dock while still under power, rather than cutting the engine and drifting to the dock.

and straight—in other respects he was a good match. His height and weight were right in the ballpark; with a baseball cap on, maybe the witnesses had misjudged his hair. The troopers seemed to remember one witness saying that the skiffman's hair was dirty; that too drove the description closer to the eyewitness accounts.

Was Moon in Craig at the time of the murders? It seemed obvious that he was, but they had to take into consideration both the fact that it was the end of the fishing season and that two other crewmen had already left the boat before the murders. Dean Moon's mother told troopers she'd spoken to Dean the Sunday before the fire and that he planned to fish that coming Tuesday. *Libby 8* crewmember Dawn Holmstrom told them she ran into Moon early Sunday evening. So the answer was, "Yes."

Was Moon an experienced fisherman? This was his third year as a professional fisherman. More important, former crewman Roy Tussing had been training Dean as the skiff operator in the weeks before he left the *Investor*. In fact, Dean held the skiff operator position at the time of the murders and fire. Did he know the Coulthursts? Yes, of course. Those three years of professional fishing were all spent on Mark Coulthurst skippered boats.

There were other, troubling allegations about Dean Moon that made it difficult to eliminate him. Did Dean Moon own a gun? Apparently so. Did he have a gun on board the *Investor*? Apparently so. And, after hearing persistent rumors about drugs on board the boat, someone came forward and implicated Dean Moon. If the informant was correct, Dean Moon was "heavy into drugs." The kinds of drugs he was "into" could have turned him into a killer.

According to the informant, who contacted Sergeant Miller in April of 1983, Moon had "ripped someone off for between $20,000 and $30,000 in cocaine money." He also was accused of stealing a half-acre of marijuana plants from a drug dealer in 1980 or 1981. Moon was allegedly capable of putting any kind of drug deal together—the informant said Moon could get cocaine, speed, PCP and psilocybin mushrooms. Not only that, but Moon was supposed to have made regular drug runs between California and Vancouver, Canada—which made him something of an international figure.

Then, in early February of 1983, Sergeant Miller got a call from

Detective Dave McNeill in Bellingham. Somebody, McNeill told him, had spotted Dean Moon. Alive. In San Francisco. When? Miller asked. Only days ago, McNeill told him.

According to court records, Miller got on the phone to talk to the man, a Bellingham fisherman. The man told Miller that he had become acquainted with "a Dean Moon kid" while they were working the Togiak herring fishery in the summer of 1982. He told him that they were tied up together ten or fifteen times during the Togiak season. Recently, the man said, he had gone to San Francisco. While he was eating dinner at Fisherman's Wharf he looked out the window and saw a young guy walk by. A young guy who reminded him of Dean Moon.

"It looked just like him," he said. "Same build, about the same, you know, same everything."

"Now, how sure are you that the person you saw was Dean Moon?" Miller asked. "Or are you sure it was him?" At that point in the investigation, Miller was accustomed to calls from people who thought they'd seen someone, whether they had actually seen someone or not. He'd come to expect it.

"Well, I'm pretty sure," the man told him. "I mean the guy has either got a double, or it was him. I mean it was that close."

"How far away from you was he?" Miller asked.

"Oh, a couple feet. Right on the sidewalk. My whole concentration was on the guy that looked like Dean."

If Dean Moon was alive, that changed everything.

Like Dean Moon, John Peel presented a difficulty. The incident that brought him to the trooper's attention was the Hill Bar sighting, but in reviewing notes from the time, Stogsdill began to question the quality of the walk-through conducted by Captain Kolivosky. The possibility remained that John Peel had seen the witnesses coming—the Hill Bar had large picture windows overlooking downtown Craig—and had simply gone into hiding while Bruce Anderson and Jan Kittleson walked through the bar. Or perhaps they were looking for someone wearing glasses—and John Peel wasn't wearing glasses. Where a suspect would have gotten glasses when he didn't wear them himself was also easy to answer. Mark Coulthurst wore glasses, in fact, wore black-rimmed glasses much like those described by Jan Kittleson.

Then there was John Peel's eerie match with every item on the blackboard grid.

Did John Peel match the physical description of the suspect? Absolutely. In the 1982 interview conducted just after the Coulthurst's memorial service in Bellingham, John Peel himself told Sgt. Miller that he was five feet, ten inches tall and weighed 150 pounds. His hair leaned toward dirty blonde. He turned 22 in May of 1982.

Was he in Craig at the time of murders? According to *Libby 8* crewmember Brian Polinkus, John Peel brought Dean Moon and Jerome Keown on board the *Libby 8* the night before the murders; the *Investor* crewmen arrived in the afternoon, around three or four o'clock, he said. Larry Demmert, Jr., Peel's skipper, also reported seeing John Peel on the Sunday before the fire, drinking beer with the crew on the deck of the *Libby 8*. Fellow crewmember Dawn Holmstrom, meanwhile, told Sergeant Miller she was with Peel on the day of the fire; the time, she thought, was 3:00 or 3:30—or whenever the fire occurred.

Peel himself told troopers that he was in Craig, on the *Libby 8*, the night of the murders.

Was John Peel an experienced fisherman? He'd fished professionally for the previous three years, two of them with Mark Coulthurst. More to the point, he had been the skiff operator on *The Kit*, the boat on which he'd fished with Mark Coulthurst.

Did he know the Coulthursts? Yes. *Did he know the crew?* Yes. Did he know the Coulthurst children? That was also a "yes." In the days after the fire he told Lisa Coulthurst, Mark's younger sister, that he had seen Kimberly and Johnny Coulthurst on the boat.

That wasn't the only evidence of Peel's proximity to the *Investor*. Troopers knew that four boats were docked around the *Investor*. They knew those boats to be the *Decade*, the *Defiant*, the *Cindy Sue* and the *Libby 8*. John Peel was on the *Libby 8*.

Then, on November 4, 1983, Stogsdill got his first bite from an article in the *Alaska Fisherman's Journal*. It came in the form of a letter addressed from Arcata, California. The letter was from a graduate student who'd been fishing in Alaska at the time of the *Investor* murders. Joe Weiss said he had just read about the unsolved homicides in the *Journal*.

He'd seen the skiffman composites in the article, he said, and something clicked. He'd seen someone resembling those composites in what looked to be the *Investor* skiff. Had seen him make a power landing at the cold storage dock. At ten o'clock on Monday morning. On Labor Day. The day before the fire.

Weiss also remembered an encounter with some guys from the *Investor* crew. He had seen them at the laundromat on Sunday night. They had scraggly beards, he said, and they were smoking pot. Stogsdill called Joe Weiss immediately. After talking to him, he decided to fly south to California.

In California, Stogsdill showed Joe Weiss two books of photographs. The first one was a photo line-up with six pictures, all headshots. That line-up now included John Peel. "If you were to have to pick a most like, which one do you think?" the sergeant asked.

"If I had to pick a most like, I'd probably, I think number three, as a most like," Weiss replied. He had barely hesitated. He liked the hair color. Liked the hair length. Liked the big bone structure and the face. He liked number three more than the other five. He liked John Peel.

10

March 1984; August 1984

Sergeant Stogsdill was now the public face of the investigation. A family man and ten-year veteran of the troopers, he was an easygoing guy, with a great sense of humor; underneath the surface was a driven, type-A personality. Like many people in law enforcement, he was a military veteran, having come almost straight out of the Air Force, where he was in the armed forces police.

Unlike Sgt. Miller, his career had only recently focused on criminal investigations. For most of his time as a trooper, Stogsdill—or "Stogs" as he was known to other troopers—was assigned to either patrol or administrative positions, including one stint as Corporal in charge of the unit that served arrest warrants. In ten more years, he was eligible for retirement; at the moment, that seemed like a long time away.

His earliest frustrations traced back to Craig, where he felt growing displeasure with the news coverage of the investigation. As he shoveled and sifted at the *Investor* scene, he grumbled about the news media. How did they seem know about everything being done in Craig? And what were the details of this case doing on CNN? Somehow, it didn't seem right that people in Miami knew as much about the case as he did. Now, a full year later, he was in a position to start turning things around.

For that to happen, Stogsdill needed to eliminate one of his two suspects. He was starting to have his doubts about Dean Moon, inspired in part by his follow up of the alleged San Francisco sighting. Accompanied by inspectors from the San Francisco homicide squad, Stogsdill walked the streets around Fisherman's Wharf and talked to the people who worked in the restaurant where the witness was eating. After a day or so, they identified one witness who had seen a man resembling the picture of Dean Moon. This witness had seen him, in fact, at about the same time the Bellingham witness had seen him. Had seen him outside the same restaurant.

But there were differences; the Bellingham witness described the young man as "clean, with a leather coat." The new witness described the same man as "a bum." He said he was "dirty." He provided Stogsdill with another lead. He said he thought the young man was looking for work with the Monterey fishermen.

Sergeant Stogsdill diligently made his way south to the Monterey peninsula and the Monterey Fisherman's Association. He interrupted their meeting to ask if anyone had seen someone resembling the photographs of Dean Moon he carried with him, but their answers were all the same. "We haven't seen this guy," they told him. "He doesn't look familiar to me," they said. Stogsdill went home empty handed, less than certain the Bellingham witness had actually seen Dean Moon.

If there was a nagging question about Moon, however, it was that he was nineteen years old at the time of the murders. Assuming he had committed those murders, and survived, he still had to go on with his life somehow, somewhere. Although not impossible, Stogsdill knew it would have been difficult for him to "go some place and assume a whole new identity and a whole new history and just actually begin again, severing all ties."

In the year following the murders, no one had heard from him. Neither his name, nor the names of his fellow crewmembers, had shown up on the national crime computer. Surviving a year on the lam seemed too much to ask of a teenager.

Inquiries with the Bellingham Police Department and drug enforcement agencies, meanwhile, revealed nothing of substance about allegations that Dean Moon was a big-time dope dealer. More than that, the guy who'd made those allegations was having credibility problems of his own. The informant claimed he'd gone to school with Moon; Stogsdill learned that the guy was six, nearly seven, years older than Moon. They hadn't gone to school together at all.

When it came to John Peel, on the other hand, small revelations kept pointing in one direction and one direction only—toward John

Peel. Once Stogsdill took over the case, Sally Coulthurst used the opportunity to repeat an earlier assertion that the *Investor* suspect's composite drawing, "looks like John Peel." She also told Stogsdill that John Peel had sold marijuana to Moon and Jerome Keown on Sunday, September 5th, the night before they died. And, she said, the last time she had seen John Peel, in the Cocoanut Grove tavern in Bellingham, she had confronted him with that information. "You know something that you haven't told the troopers," she had told him, referring to the marijuana sale. "Next time they're in town," she admonished him, "'you better tell them.'"

Even as she said that, Sally Coulthurst recognized the complications it brought: John Peel's mother, Marilyn, had baked her daughter Lisa's wedding cake; what was she going to do when it came time to return the cake platters and decorations? She didn't know.

Former crewman Roy Tussing told troopers about an incident involving John Peel on Mark's previous boat, *The Kit*. The crew decided to have a barbecue on one of the uninhabited islands that dot the Inside Passage in southeast Alaska; a fair amount of liquor was consumed while they waited for the food. After a while, they noticed Peel passed out in the galley. They thought, why not tie him to the table? That's what they did, taking a length of rope and tying his feet to the legs of the table. Then they wondered whether they could get his hands, too. They had to do it without waking him. When they were done, they went back to their barbecue.

An hour or so later, they heard angry shouts coming from inside *The Kit*. John Peel had come to his senses. "Get me out of here you assholes," he shouted. "Get me out of here."

Only one crewman volunteered to help. Dean Moon. He brought Peel a knife and was ready to cut the ropes. Somehow, though, the captive wasn't grateful. John Peel started blaming his rescuer; told him he would kick his ass when he got out of the ropes. Moon wisely cut one hand free, then put the knife on the galley table. "Cut your ownself free," he told him.

They also came across another tidbit from a Bellingham fisherman, who told them that Peel hitched a ride north in 1982 on his fishing boat, the *Cleveland*. During the long ride up the Inside Passage, the fisherman said, Peel kept at the liquor. One night, while quite drunk,

Peel badmouthed Mark Coulthurst in the strongest possible terms. Peel meant it, the fisherman insisted. There was anger in his voice.

Based on that tidbit, and the new information from Sally Coulthurst, Stogsdill demanded that Peel come to the Bellingham police department for another interview. Once there, Peel confirmed that he'd sold marijuana to Dean Moon, and that he'd hitched a ride north on the *Cleveland*. When troopers asked him about the *Investor* fire, he said he had gone out on the *Cindy Sue*, which belonged to Larry Demmert, Jr.'s dad, while the *Investor* was burning.

"How big was the fire when you got there?" Stogsdill asked him.

"All the bulwarks were burned back," Peel replied, referring to the raised area that extended around the deck of the boat. But Stogsdill knew better. The bulwarks hadn't burned at all. Peel also told Stogsdill that the *Investor* was tied up at South Cove, when in fact it was tied up at North Cove. John Peel's statements were at odds with what troopers already knew. Why? What was he trying to hide?

Even though Stogsdill had narrowed things down to a single suspect, he still had a problem. It all started at Fish Egg Island. Had the killer succeeded in sinking the *Investor* as intended, the bodies would likely have been in-place and intact. Bullet holes and trajectories could have been traced, bullet fragments or casings recovered, untold evidence discovered; altogether it would have been a richer and much more intact crime scene. When that admittedly amateurish first pass at hiding the crime failed, the killer had to switch to Plan B.

The fire was devastating. It lingered for two days, steadily compromising evidence as it continued. After tamping it down on the evening of September 7th, troopers arrived the next day to learn that it was still flaring up. A firefighting helicopter was brought in to dump seawater on the *Investor*'s hull, dipped its five hundred-gallon bucket into the sea and, hovering about a hundred feet over the vessel, unceremoniously dumped its entire load on the still-smoking hulk. The fire proved surprisingly resistant; only after several fly-bys was it brought down.

Even with that, it wasn't until they used foam fire retardant that they extinguished the *Investor* fire once and for all.

Compounding that existential difficulty, the case had simply gone on too long without a resolution. Witnesses were originally shown lineup photos without John Peel. Eighteen months on, each passing day challenged their memories, threatened to make them more tentative, more fragile. The fear associated with an unsolved crime of this magnitude troubled their brains and their emotions.

In an eight-page memo to Ketchikan prosecutor Mary Anne Henry, Stogsdill addressed those concerns. Even as he named John Peel his chief suspect, he admitted there was "no case" without Peel's confession and additional supporting evidence. "There are no other suspects in this case, however remote," he wrote.

The memo used the twelve-item list developed during the "Anniversary Meeting" as rationale for making John Peel their prime suspect. It also listed seven reasons to believe Peel was not involved: he had no obvious motive, was not identified by witnesses and said he was in bed that night by 6:00 p.m. because he was "stoned."

"Suffice it to say that a confession with collaborating [sic] facts is imperative to conclude this case," Stogsdill wrote. "Without it, there is no case."

Stogsdill's plan for dealing with those problems was two-fold.

First, they were going to solidify the coterie of eyewitnesses by bringing up Joe Weiss for an in-person surveillance trip with trooper Sergeants Flothe and Galyan. They found John Peel in Friday Harbor, a small town in the San Juan Islands, just west of Bellingham, where he was part of a crew from Builders Concrete, putting in a new float.[8] During breakfast at a donut shop, Joe Weiss thought he saw someone he recognized. "I want to get a better look at those two guys," Weiss muttered under his breath, nodding toward Peel and the guy sitting next to him, an unrelated co-worker from Bellingham, who was wearing a *Moose Head* beer baseball cap.

Weiss got up to get another cup of coffee and, on the way back to the booth, paused to get a closer look at the two young men. Ten minutes later, he repeated the exam, again stopping to catch a close-up. He wouldn't get another opportunity. The young men left just as quickly as they came.

Although Flothe and Galyan knew that Peel was probably headed for the harbor, they took a meandering route to the waterfront. They

8 After years of failure as a commercial fisherman, John Peel had recently taken a job building concrete floats in Bellingham. He was not making much money, but the job provided his family with health benefits.

were diverted by the pleasure boats and fishing vessels that crowded one side of the moorage. As they neared the harbor, though, they found it more deserted. Two small skiffs bobbed next to the dock. Sitting in one of them was John Peel. John Peel and the guy with the *Moose Head* beer cap.

As the trio turned and headed toward the two skiffs, Weiss, who had been trailing the troopers, found himself in the lead. He took advantage of his freedom. Independent of any urging by Flothe and Galyan, Weiss walked within twenty feet of the skiffs. He yelled out, "You going fishing?"

According to court records, only one guy responded: the guy who was expertly running the boat.

"I wish we were going fishing," John Peel yelled back. "We're putting the new float in."

As the troopers struggled up the hill, back to their motel, Joe Weiss spoke out. He told them that the two guys in the skiff looked a lot like the skiffman he'd seen in Craig. A lot. Of the two, he liked the guy in the front of the skiff the best, the guy with the *Moose Head* cap. "The one," Flothe thought, "who was not John Peel." Weiss quickly added that the two guys in the skiff looked a lot alike; they looked so similar, he said, that they looked like brothers. So there it was; not the homerun they wanted, but a solid hit into the outfield.

Step two in the plan was to sit down and have a long talk with John Peel. When they talked to him, they were going to confront him. Stogsdill was ready to gamble that Peel would break down once faced with the reality of his acts; he would break down and he would confess.

To strengthen their chances, Stogsdill started working on Peel's psyche. From the moment he returned to Peel's hometown in late March, he gave the *Bellingham Herald* story after story about the *Investor*. They were also getting airtime: local television station KVOS broadcast excerpts from a trooper-produced movie that showed the burning *Investor* and asked anyone with knowledge of the crime to step forward. By week's end, the station agreed to show the 28-minute film in its entirety.

The tone of the media blitz was set, however, by the opening piece in the *Herald*. In a March 20th front-page story, staff writer Donald Tapperson wrote that four Alaska State Troopers had arrived in town, "to pursue their continuing investigation of the mass murder and arson aboard the purse seiner *Investor*."

"We're not letting up," the article said, quoting Stogsdill. "That's why we're here."

The next day the *Herald* ran another *Investor*-related story. Starting with the headline, it was apparent that Stogsdill was tightening the screws. "Police uncover a new witness in *Investor* case," the headline announced.

"A new witness in the *Investor* mass murder and arson case has emerged in the last month," the article revealed, "with fresh information that has given the Alaska State Troopers renewed hope for a solution, according to the head of the investigation. That, coupled with the recent development of highly detailed 'behavioral' and 'abilities' profiles of the wanted man—and speculations about his motive for the crimes—has led the team's leader, Sgt. James Stogsdill, to believe that 'we're on our way to the end. A solution is closer than ever before.' "

In the article, Stogsdill asked local fishermen to review a checklist of the suspect's behavioral and abilities profiles—and asked them to compare those traits with characteristics of fishermen they had known or met. "I'm not sure we're talking about many people," Stogsdill noted. "All of the characteristics may apply only to one person."

In a related piece, which featured a brooding picture of an obviously weary Stogsdill, the sergeant provided a detailed description of their suspect. This was the description intended to break loose a few phone calls. "I'm here to get people to point the finger at people," Stogsdill announced.

The profile that emerged was, not surprisingly, consistent with the profile troopers developed during the so-called "Anniversary Meeting" in Craig. White male, in his late teens or early twenties, a fisherman. Someone with "an unsteady job history." Someone who had encounters with the police, though not for major crimes. "Drunk driving," Stogsdill suggested. "Petty crimes."

In other words, John Peel.

11

Bellingham, Washington
March 1984

A t the direction of the troopers, John Peel arrived at the Bellingham police station a little bit after three in the afternoon, ostensibly to discuss the case. Alaska State Trooper Sergeant Daryl Galyan, a veteran of the Robert Hansen serial murder case, led him to the interview room in the detective division.[9] Court records describe it as a cramped, L-shaped room, barely six feet wide and ten feet long. The biggest thing in it was a rugged table, on which were perched a microphone and several newspaper clippings. Galyan instructed Peel to take a seat.

The troopers didn't start the interview. They let him sit. Alone. The purpose wasn't so much to make him stew as to make sure he saw the news clippings. "We know all about you," the *Bellingham Herald* articles seemed to say. "We know what you did."

The game plan had Peel going up against Sergeants Flothe and Galyan. Sergeant Stogsdill was sitting on the other side of the one-way glass, manning the tape recorder. Next to him in the recording booth was Ketchikan prosecuting attorney Mary Anne Henry. Henry had flown down to Bellingham because she was curious—she wanted to see John Peel first hand—and, if he confessed, she was ready to get the arrest warrant and prepare extradition papers.

Once the troopers were convinced that Peel had taken a good look

---

9   Both Sergeant Galyan and Sergeant Flothe had worked on the Robert Hansen serial murder case; Sergeant Flothe was the lead investigator and played a critical role in bringing Hansen to justice.

at the articles, everything swung into action. "Oh, you're here?" Flothe said as he peeked into the room, pretending to be surprised.

"Yeah," Peel answered. He asked if he could smoke a cigarette; the troopers told him no, the room was too small. Galyan immediately moved to the formalities; he pointed out the microphone, and got Peel's agreement to be taped. Flothe then read him his rights. Peel agreed to talk, without a lawyer. Then the troopers maneuvered themselves into position.

Sergeant Flothe, whose designated task was to keep a watchful eye on these proceedings, pulled back a little, so that his chair was about three feet from the table. Galyan seemed to scoot his chair up a little closer to John Peel as he began to speak. The move was subtle, almost imperceptible. "Okay," Galyan intoned as the interview got underway. "John, like I say, this has been a long, involved case, and hundreds of people have been talked to."

"Is that right?" Peel answered.

Compared to the two troopers, John Peel was a small man. Beneath his fisherman's garb he was well muscled, a man who worked with his hands. Galyan did not rush to a confrontation. Instead, he had Peel explain what he was doing in Craig at the time of the murders—for the most part, this was familiar territory and Peel gave them familiar answers. He was fishing on the *Libby 8* that summer, he told them. Their boat was tied up behind the *Investor*. He had worked for Mark Coulthurst. Knew some of the *Investor* crew. Smoked pot with them, drank a few beers. So far, everything was routine, almost conversational. But soon, Galyan pushed things in another direction. He asked John Peel if he had been reading the newspapers.

Peel admitted to reading one of the articles they'd so thoughtfully left out for him. The one that said the troopers had a new witness. Galyan jumped on the opportunity offered by Peel's offhand admission. "Do you recognize either one of us," he asked. Peel said he thought he recognized Sergeant Flothe.

"You know," Galyan announced, "one of the reasons that you probably recognize him, and I thought maybe you might recognize me, is that yesterday I was sitting in San Juan."

"Oh, you were?" John Peel's response was matter-of-fact, even somewhat knowing.

"I was sitting on the dock," Galyan continued, "and Glenn was sitting on the dock with me. And there was another guy on the dock with me."

"Yeah," Peel answered.

"All right. If you'll bear with me," Galyan announced, "I'm going to tell you a little story, and I'm going to brief you on why I'm down here. I want you to listen closely, because this may very seriously affect your life. That witness that they're talking about in the paper identified…"

"Identified me," Peel said, interrupting Galyan. He had guessed correctly.

"…you as the person that came off the skiff from the *Investor* the morning that all those people were killed," Galyan continued, finishing the sentence.

"Okay, then that's all I'm going to say. I want to talk to a lawyer then, you know," Peel said, letting out a nervous laugh. Then he, too, turned serious. "Are you pressing charges on me or…"

No, Flothe told him, they were not pressing charges. "I was just telling you a story," Galyan declared. Flothe chimed in that Peel could have an attorney if he wanted one.

"This comes as a surprise," Peel finally responded. "Scary." But he told the troopers he wanted to hear Galyan's story, even as he mumbled, "what a rush."

"There were four witnesses," Galyan revealed, upping the ante. Three of them, he said, had tentatively identified Peel as the skiffman. Peel asked what "tentatively" meant. Galyan told him that three of the witnesses had only seen photographic line-ups and hadn't seen him in person.

"I knew you were there," Peel suddenly responded, revealing that he had seen them at Friday Harbor. "I thought you were coming over to question me."

"Okay," Galyan shot back, raising the confrontation factor another notch. "Of the multitude of facts that have come to light in this case, John, it leads me to believe that you're involved up to your ears in this thing. There's been a lot of speculation about motive, John. Why—why did this happen?"

"You tell me," the young man said, suddenly brash and on the offensive.

"Let me tell you something, John," Galyan insisted. "The case is coming very quickly to a conclusion here."

"Oh, you think you got your man, right?" Peel said, his voice drenched in sarcasm.

"I didn't say that. I said the case is going to come to a conclusion. All right? Don't put words in my mouth."

"What do you think the motive was?" Peel asked, finally managing to string more than a couple of words together.

"What do I think the motive was? Do you want me to lay it out for you?" Galyan asked. Taking his cue from Peel, Galyan launched into an elaborate explanation. He put his theory in front of John Peel like an old uncle telling a childhood tale. He left little to the imagination.

"My theory," he began, "based on everything that the investigation has shown, on eyewitness testimony and this sort of thing, is that I know that you have worked for Mark in the past. I know Mark was—how should you describe him? Very difficult at times. Probably in the fishing terms around the dock, he was an asshole as a skipper. The next thing I know is that he won't even let you work for him. All right? Then you wind up—you're trying to get over there to Craig simply so that you can get a job and you can work and support your family. All right?"

"All right," Peel said, going along with the narration.

"You ask Mark just for a lousy ride from Ketchikan to Craig, and what does he tell you? Hey, he can't be bothered with you. 'I'm not even going that way.' The guy lies to you."

"Yeah," Peel said, still listening.

"Then the end of the fishing season comes along," Galyan continued. "It's Mark's birthday. He goes out to the restaurant with his wife and kids and the family and whatever. All right? I think—my theory, John, is that you bought maybe a bottle with your last few bucks before you got paid. You might have gone over to the *Investor* with the guys, had a couple of drinks. I think you probably wanted to wish Mark maybe a happy birthday. He ain't there. Dean and Jerome and the rest of them are. You guys are all buddies. All right?"

Galyan paused for emphasis, but he was far from finished. He was just getting warmed up. He was working his way toward the act of murder.

"The hours drag by," Galyan continued. "The next thing you know it's 10:30, 11 :00 o'clock at night. Finally—you know, you guys have been drinking and talking and having a good time, and kind of wasted. Finally, around 10:30, 11:00 o'clock, here comes Mark, you know. You're happy to see him. You like the guy, you know. You worked for him. All right?"

"Yeah," John Peel said, staying noncommittal.

"He berates you in front of your friends. Maybe he orders you off the boat or whatever. I don't know, you know—theory, right? The next thing I know, John, is all of a sudden the gun is there, things go bad. Didn't mean to do it. Okay? All you meant to do is—is to defend your own honor so you don't look like a wimp in front of your friends."

"John, I'm telling you right now, I think that's what happened. It was an accident, didn't mean for it to happen. It was," Galyan said, snapping his fingers, "Bang, over, and what can you do? You can't go back and change the past. All you can do is try to go forward, right?"

While Peel listened patiently, Galyan enlarged his theory to encompass the days following the murders. He spoke of the failed attempt to sink the vessel. He spoke of the fire. Both times, Galyan declared, people had seen him.

Finished with his theory, Galyan pushed for resolution. "My problem, and the reason that Jim [Stogsdill] let me come down here," he declared, "is because I don't—you know, I don't believe in injustice. If you did this for a robbery motive, hoping to get a bunch of bucks and whatever, I think the guy is a terrible, bad person. But if that's not the case, John, I think everybody has a right to know that that isn't what happened, that it was an accident, that nobody meant for anybody to get hurt. Don't you agree with me?"

"I think you're nuts, man," Peel answered.

"I am not nuts, John," Galyan countered.

"I don't—geez, I just can't believe this."

"Let me tell you something here, John," Galyan said. "This is all going to come down around your neck. I want you to listen very closely. You're a young man. You've got your whole life in front of you."

"I don't know what to say," Peel muttered. He was nearly speechless. He was swallowing his words. He was surrounded. Galyan wasn't letting up. "John, you're not a bad guy. All right? You've had to live with this for a long time, and I don't think it's been easy."

"Jesus Christ," Peel exclaimed, the words spitting out of his mouth. "I can't believe that you guys think I did it, man." He was shaking his head, trying to throw back Galyan's words in a rush of disbelief.

"Listen to me," Galyan demanded. "I'm not down here to bullshit you."

"Yeah," Peel insisted, his voice burning with anger. "I think you guys are trying to put an end to this case because it's taking so much fucking time."

"No."

"You got to find somebody," Peel blurted out.

"If I ask you to take a polygraph," Galyan asked, "would you take one? Do you know what a polygraph is?"

"Well, right now," John Peel admitted, "my heart's pounding so bad I can't believe it."

"We'll let you calm down and have a cigarette while you're—if that's the case," Galyan pronounced.

"I think I'd better talk to a lawyer before I do that," Peel replied; but he seemed uncertain what he should do next. "Okay. I'll—yeah, I'll take one," Peel said. The change of mind was sudden. Startling.

"John, you've got to make up your mind," Galyan answered.

"I'm scared, man. I am scared," Peel finally revealed. "I can't believe what you think I did in there."

"Well, I'm offering you a polygraph," Galyan said.

"It'll clear it up once and for all," Sergeant Flothe assured him.

"Yeah. Okay," Peel said, warming to the prospect. "You bet."

They led John Peel to the polygraph room. There, he would have the electrodes attached to his body. There, Detective McNeill would start asking him more questions. John Peel would try to give them the answers.

If anything, the polygraph room at the Bellingham Police station seemed even smaller—more claustrophobic—than the interview room. To make matters worse, there was the uncomfortable prospect of being hooked up to a tangle of polygraph wires and electrodes. The probing questions. The underlying sense of distrust. The irony that, even if the test subject passed the exam, the results could not be admitted in court. No one willingly submitted to this process; only fools did so without their lawyer present.

In a rambling interview that seemed to cover every phase of John Peel's short life, Detective McNeill laid the groundwork for his most probing questions. In the end everything came down to a few responses.

"Did you murder Mark Coulthurst?" McNeill asked after they were deep into the exam.

"No," Peel replied.

"Do you know for sure who murdered Mark Coulthurst?"

"No," Peel said.

"You have no idea?"

John Peel shook his head. "No," he was gesturing. "No."

"Did you set the fire that burned the *Investor*?"

"No," Peel once more replied.

John Peel's denials notwithstanding, McNeill wasn't impressed. His reading of the polygraph charts told him Peel had been "deceptive" during the interview. Peel insisted he'd been telling the truth and wanted a chance to explain. Not only that, but he wanted to take the polygraph examination again.

Daryl Galyan was less than receptive to Peel's request. He'd looked at the charts, he told Peel. He hadn't seen anything that would cause him to think the results would change. "You lied on the polygraph," Galyan insisted, taking a seat next to Peel. "I can take those charts to any polygraphist, even a first-week student, John, and I can lay those on a table. All right?"

Peel mumbled a complaint under his breath. His words were lost in Galyan's speech, however, and only belatedly did the cop realize that their suspect was saying something.

"I'm sorry, I didn't hear that," Galyan said, stopping himself short.

"I said, 'Well, the machine can't work that well then, because I wasn't lying.'"

"Well, I hate to pop your little bubble, John," Galyan said, leaning closer, "but the polygraph does work. There are places in there that you are truthful. It shows that. There are places in there that you are not truthful, and it shows that. John, there's no question in my mind that you did this thing. The question that I have in my mind is: are you sorry that you got involved?"

"So you're expecting me to say I'm sorry for something I didn't do?" Peel asked.

"All I'm doing is talking to you," Galyan insisted. "All I'm doing is telling you exactly where I'm coming from and exactly why. John, there's no doubt about it, that you did this."

"Oh, my God," he said, the bravado gone.

"The only question is 'Why?' And we're right back to the same issue here. Okay?"

"No. I think it's about time I got a lawyer, if… if there's no doubt in your mind."

"There's no doubt in my mind, John," Galyan said. "I told you that. If you want an attorney, we told you four or five times earlier, walk out of here. I'll tell you this, though, John, that if at any time you wanted to talk, you wanted to try to square the thing away, if you wanted…"

"That's what I wanted to do…" Peel blurted out. "I wanted to square it away with you."

"Now, I don't want to hear that," Galyan responded gruffly. "I've got twelve-feet of chart paper, John, that's absolutely full of lies. All you have to do is be honest with me and say, 'Daryl, I've got a problem. Can you help?' "

"Hey, you're the one that's got a problem," Peel said sarcastically. "You've got the wrong guy." His attitude—and voice—turned blunt and insistent. "Now, I want to resolve this thing right now."

"You're not telling me the truth, John," Galyan shot back. "It's as simple as that. All right?"

"Okay," Peel shot back. "Then I'm going to walk out of here right now."

"Sorry. I've tried to help you," Galyan insisted. "The time is now 6:21."

But John Peel was frozen in place. He didn't know what to expect next. He had to ask the obvious question. "You going to arrest me or…" he said, his voice fading into nothingness.

They had reached an impasse, so Galyan threw another tidbit into the mix. Peel, it seemed, had come to the police station with a tape that, he said, had been made aboard *The Kit*. After repeated listenings, conducted while Peel was being polygraphed, the troopers managed to make out a few words. Someone was heard saying, "Mark." And then "passed out." And "needle in his arm." They also heard a drug word.

74

"Coke." Galyan had no idea that this was a joke tape made by Roy Tussing and the crew of *The Kit*, but he still confronted him.

"Remember that tape you gave me?" Galyan asked. "I've listened to that tape a dozen times. I can—I, in my own mind, I think the reason you gave us that tape is you're trying to tell us something. And I'm not sure what, but from listening to that very tape—I listened to it a dozen times—I can form a mental picture of those guys partying aboard that boat.'"

"Yeah," Peel replied in the same monotone he had used during much of the interview.

"I can just take that tape and say, 'Now, this is the crew of the *Investor* making it into port, end of the season,'" he opined, getting the boat name wrong. "Irene and the kids are leaving the next day, and they're whooping it up and having a good time. Mark's out to dinner, but Mark comes back and something goes wrong..."

"Oh, I can see I need some help..." Peel said. "You guys wasted a lot of effort."

"No we didn't," Galyan declared. "You can stand there and attempt to—you know, you can tell the lies all you want. It doesn't alter a thing."

"Boy, you guys are intimidating me," Peel blurted out. Galyan had moved within inches of the young man; at times, their knees were scraping. His face seemed even closer. "You guys are... You come up this far away from my face."

"Well, hey," Galyan said, raising his voice another notch. "I'm not about to talk to you from ten feet across the room."

"Is there anything that you want us to do?" Flothe asked. "It's up to you. Now, we're the police, right?"

"Well, okay. Well, wait a day," the fisherman told them. "I'll try it again tomorrow, you know, because I'm too tense. After all, that gives me a day to think about it..."

"That sort of thing doesn't make me any difference, John," said Galyan. "The only time that a re-exam does any good is when it would lead to a psychological reason, you've got a mental case in there."

"Maybe I do have a mental case," Peel offered.

"Maybe you do, I don't know. Okay? All you want to do is just jump up and down and say that you talked to me."

"Well, if you were in my shoes—innocent—what would you do?"

Peel's response had a bit of everything in it: part pleading, part fear, part anxiety.

"If I was in your shoes and I was innocent, I wouldn't be here, John," Galyan declared. "But I'm not in your shoes and you're not innocent. That's the problem that I'm faced with here. I took a week off to come down here…"

"You're in… you're in my shoes and innocent, you wouldn't be here now?" Peel asked, incredulous.

"That's right."

For the first time in a while, John Peel stood up. His move was deliberate, determined and definitive. "See you later," he declared and, pulling up all his courage, he walked out the door.

12

Faced with John Peel's unwillingness to break under their pressure, the troopers dove into the mundane. On the Sunday following the interview, they cleaned up the mess they'd made at the Bellingham police station. The work was mindless and would have stayed that way, save for Larry Demmert, Jr. His curiosity aroused by the rush of articles in the *Herald*, the *Libby 8* skipper insinuated himself into the police station uninvited, before anyone was ready for him. The cops listened to his concerns, speculated briefly on the idea that John Peel was a murderer, and shooed him away.

The troopers were, however, very much interested in John Peel's crewmates on the *Libby 8*. If they persisted, maybe Peel's friends would implicate him. If they kept after them, maybe his friends would stop providing what they saw as nothing more than false alibis.

With their day of rest behind them, the troopers circled back to Larry Demmert; this time they were ready to talk to him. Court documents reveal that Peel's skipper told them several things they'd never heard before. He told them Peel claimed to have spent the night of the murders "at his girlfriend's house." Demmert added that, as he returned to the *Libby 8* that evening, he saw someone clambering onto the *Investor*.

"The guy looked like a dirty old fisherman to me," Demmert said.

Demmert also recalled that Peel was nowhere to be seen the following morning. He remembered that, he said, because he was mad that no one besides Dawn Holmstrom had shown up to help untie the boat and move it to the cannery. Peel, it seemed to Demmert, was more concerned about making arrangements to fly out of Craig. Demmert said those plans were "kind of an iffy thing" and characterized them as "last minute."

On the day of the fire, the skipper added, Peel turned down an offer to ride out to the scene on the *Cindy Sue*, Demmert's father's boat. Demmert thought Peel's refusal was "really strange." In the interview, Demmert stated, "I said, 'What the hell's with you, don't you want to see the fire?' He said, 'No, I don't want to see it.' "

Asked to describe his crewman, a man he had known since grade school, Demmert said he was "a good guy sometimes, but then he'll turn around and screw you, right away. Like he'll say one thing to you and run around and totally do the opposite thing. He gets a wild look in his eyes. Dawn knows that, can verify that. He gets a wild look in his eyes sometimes."

Could he imagine Peel committing murder? Referring to a conversation he'd had with Sergeant Stogsdill just the day before, Demmert allowed as to how he could imagine a set of circumstances which would have led Peel to murder.

"Do you think Peel has the ability under the right circumstances— maybe under the influence of drugs and booze—to do something like this?" Flothe pressed.

"You mean crazy enough to kill somebody?" Demmert asked.

"Yeah," Flothe answered.

Larry Demmert, Jr., paused. He was thinking hard about his friend. "I think he probably could be the sort of person that could do something like that, myself. That's why it bothers me so much."

Unlike Larry Demmert, Dawn Holmstrom did not face the troopers by herself. Larry Demmert stayed behind and the troopers interviewed them together. Even a stranger could tell these two were old friends. Sometimes they finished each other's sentences, like an old married couple.

Holmstrom started by confirming her skipper's assertion that John Peel had not returned to the boat on the day of the murders. She didn't remember seeing him, in fact, until the next day. The first time she saw him, she said, was on her way to the bank with Demmert's underage girlfriend. "That's when we saw all the smoke," she added.

Pressed for details, Holmstrom was initially uncertain when she'd seen the fire. After thinking about it, she indicated that she'd first seen the fire when "it was really going." The sky was black with smoke, she added, describing it as "a big puff." Larry Demmert, meanwhile, returned to the thought that "it was weird" that John Peel didn't want to go see the *Investor* fire.

More interesting to Holmstrom, however, was Peel's psyche. He wanted to quit fishing, she said. "All the time, he's going, 'Dawn, I want to quit, I just want to fly home, I just want to get out of here.'" The reason, she said, was that they weren't catching many fish. Taking her insights a step further, she said Peel "was getting depressed" toward the end of the season. Then, on the day after the fire, Holmstrom ran into Peel at Ruth Ann's in Craig. They had a beer, she seemed to recall. "And John was really upset and he was crying. He made me cry."

"What was he crying about?" Flothe immediately asked.

"He just couldn't believe how anyone could do that," Dawn revealed, then mumbled that she couldn't believe it either.

The troopers finished their Bellingham sojourn with Brian Polinkus, the final member of the *Libby 8* crew. They began by reading him his Miranda rights. They followed that with a reference to "discrepancies" they'd uncovered, and the possibility that some of the witnesses might be lying.

The discrepancies went right to the question of marijuana, not just because of the "drug angle," but because Polinkus appeared to be protecting his friend, John Peel. Poor Brian didn't know that Peel had already told them about the marijuana. He insisted that neither he nor John Peel had any dope, that they had gotten some from Dean Moon and Jerome Keown.

"We were all out," he said, "and they were just offering to smoke some with us."

Thinking that Polinkus was lying to protect himself from the legal ramifications of drug possession, Flothe tried to reassure him. "Okay. We're not here investigating a marijuana case, so I hope you realize that."

"Yeah," Polinkus replied. "Well, it's legal up there anyway."

But if Polinkus was protecting Peel from drug charges, he wasn't protecting him from everything. He confirmed Demmert's recollection about where Peel claimed to have spent the night of the murders. "I wasn't with John the whole night," Polinkus said, "because he didn't come back that night. The next morning when I saw him, you know, I asked him, 'Where in the hell were you?'" Peel told him he'd been with his Craig girlfriend.

"Sunday... Sunday's the night that John didn't come back?" Flothe asked.

"Sunday's the night John didn't come back," the young crewman confirmed. Then he seemed confused, because he added, "The night before the boat burned, is the night John didn't come back." Polinkus seemed confused about other things as well. He seemed to think Peel had gone out to see the fire on the *Cindy Sue*, though Larry Demmert thought otherwise. He also seemed to think he'd seen Peel on the Craig boardwalk, an hour before the fire. Later, he recalled seeing Peel on the boardwalk *after* going out to the fire.

"Then we came back and that's when I saw him," Polinkus recalled. "I said, 'Well, shit, John, what do you think about it,' you know? And he just... He said, 'I don't know.' And he goes, 'I wouldn't be surprised if they're all dead,' you know."

Flothe reminded the fisherman that, earlier in the interview, he'd described that conversation differently. In his initial description, Polinkus had Peel speculating that the victims had been shot.

"Shot, yeah," Polinkus said. "And I go, 'Well, shit,' you know, 'what do you...?' Because it was in the daytime. And then later on, when they brought the bodies in that evening, you know, and I heard that they were shot, I thought, 'Jesus Christ.' Because that guy told me he wouldn't be surprised if that's what had happened."

"Sometimes two plus two makes four," Flothe suggested.

"Yeah. And I... But I... I... You know, I don't think, you know, I just really don't think John would do it," Polinkus insisted. "You know, I've lived with him. I know him. He's just... He's not that crazy."

If the troopers had a problem with Brian Polinkus—and they had several—it was that he didn't seem to remember what he was doing the Sunday night before the murders. Try as he may, Brian Polinkus could not remember who he had been with, or what he had been doing, that crucial Sunday night. Despite that blank, Polinkus seemed absolutely certain he'd never been on board the *Investor*. After twice catching him lying about alcohol use on the *Libby 8*, Flothe asked him to take a polygraph test.

"We just sort of have a problem with you not remembering where you're at," Flothe told him, "but definitely knowing that you have never been on the *Investor*."

"Right," he assured them. "I'd do it."

Before they had him take the polygraph exam, however, the troopers gave Brian some photographs to look at. Pictures of the *Libby 8*'s crew, of John Peel. They had him identifying clothing and hats—John Peel's clothing, John Peel's hat. Then, at 4:39 p.m., they went off the record. They didn't come back on the record until 7:37 p.m. In the intervening three hours, Brian Polinkus had an epiphany. Faced with the prospect of the polygraph—whose mere psychological effect usually outweighs its scientific capabilities—Brian Polinkus rolled over.

"We just have a couple of questions to ask you," Flothe intoned when the tape started rolling. "Perhaps you'd like to re-clarify or straighten up the matter concerning the marijuana. I think perhaps we should do that before you leave. Why don't you tell me the truth about that?"

"Okay," Polinkus said, sheepishly. "Well, John got some pot in the mail and, uh, he sold a bag to them and that's where they got the pot that they were smoking."

"See, that one little lie," Flothe lectured him, "could have led us off astray. Terribly."

"Yeah, I know. I realize that," Brian apologized. "I just don't want to, you know, John to get arrested for marijuana selling out there."

"As far as we're concerned," Flothe assured him, "that's insignificant compared to murder."

The transaction, according to Polinkus, took place in the fo'c's'le of the *Libby 8*. Polinkus wasn't sure how much pot they bought, but said it was a cash transaction. Maybe two or four hundred dollars had changed hands. He thought Dean Moon was the one with the cash, but wasn't sure. The marijuana, he said, had been sent up from Washington State. He thought Peel's wife had sent it. But with those questions, the interview came to a sudden end. Brian Polinkus was trying to remember additional details, and he couldn't.

The troopers had by now had their fill of Bellingham and the *Libby 8* crew. If one thing emerged from John Peel's flaky friends, it was that Peel had been missing on the Sunday night before the murders. Missing and unaccounted for. So Stogsdill headed north again. Back to Craig. Because no matter how far they got in their investigation, it seemed everything came back to Craig.

There, they talked to John Peel's girlfriend—erstwhile girlfriend, in fact. She told Stogsdill she'd never been on the *Investor* in her life. That she didn't smoke pot. She also told troopers that she'd broken up with Peel when she found out he was married. She'd broken up with him some time before the murders. That, in short, she was not and could not be his alibi for the night of the murders.

On the 14th day of August, another development crossed their radar screens: the coroner ruled that Dean Moon and Chris Heyman were presumed dead in a homicide and were last seen alive in Craig, Alaska, on September 5, 1982. The ruling came as a great relief to the families. Ruth Moon, especially, felt vindicated. She had never thought her son a murderer, had always believed Sergeant Miller had gone down a blind alley when he kept pointing the finger at Dean.

It took until the end of August before Stogsdill took a plane flight south. But, he didn't fly to Seattle. He didn't fly to Bellingham. He flew to Ketchikan. He read through all the interviews again—including their latest updates. This time Ketchikan prosecuting attorney Mary Anne Henry was with him. Based on what they read, Stogsdill reached two conclusions. First, he decided he had enough against John Peel to obtain an arrest warrant for murder. Mary Anne Henry concurred. Secondly, he reiterated the view that his best chance for a favorable disposition rested with John Peel's confession.

"I want to go back down to Bellingham and talk to him," he told Mary Anne Henry.

They would go to Bellingham, the prosecuting attorney agreed. They would also have a backup plan, in case John Peel didn't confess. The prosecuting attorney's office would prepare an arrest warrant in advance and could get it to a judge the minute they needed to put the warrant into action.

There was some precedent for this approach. Two years earlier, troopers had confronted serial killer Robert Hansen with allegations of his involvement in the deaths of topless dancers and prostitutes in Anchorage. Hansen didn't confess until after his arrest, when the impact of a trial on his family hit him full force.

By the time they arrived in Bellingham, it was September 5th. Two years prior to the day, Mark Coulthurst, his family and his crew were murdered on the *Investor*. It was time to bring everything home.

13

Bellingham, Washington
September 7, 1984

Sgt. Stogsdill made his move on a Friday, two days after arriving back in town. He grabbed Detective McNeill and they found John Peel at his house. They told him they needed to talk. Peel agreed but said he was eating dinner. He wanted them to come back in an hour. Stogsdill, not wanting to alarm their only suspect, agreed to come back later.

The two officers wasted time cruising Bellingham, but kept their word; they returned to Peel's house in an hour. Just as they neared the house, however, they spotted his truck going down a cross street. A visit to his residence confirmed their suspicions: John Peel was no longer home. Stogsdill and McNeill didn't see him the rest of the day.

The next day, they staked out Peel's home. When he got in his little truck and left, they followed him to a gas station and then downtown. When Peel parked his truck, Stogsdill had McNeill stop just behind him. Before Peel got out of the truck, Stogsdill was at his window.

"Can I talk to you for a minute," the trooper asked.

John Peel rolled the window down, but court records indicate that his answer was abrupt. "I don't have anything to say," he told the trooper. Then he announced that he was going to call his attorney.

"Tell me who your attorney is," Stogsdill offered. "I'd like to call him and talk to him and set up a meeting between us."

John Peel was having none of the sergeant's counterproposals. He rolled up the window.

"Can you give me a reason why you're innocent?" Stogsdill asked as John Peel started his truck and drove away. Stogsdill went back to Detective McNeill's waiting police car. The time had come, he decided, to arrest John Peel for murder.

They called in the warrant on Saturday night. Dave McNeill confirmed the warrant's existence on Sunday morning and Mary Anne Henry promised she'd be there by Sunday night with the warrant in hand. McNeill and Stogsdill spent their Sunday staked out at John Peel's house. On this particular Sabbath, however, Peel followed his parents to their house and spent the day with them. Stogsdill didn't like the prospects. He didn't want the complications sure to follow an attempt to arrest him in front of his family. He wanted Peel by himself, so he'd have one more chance to talk to him.

By Monday, September 10th, Stogsdill had been in town five days and John Peel was still on the street. That morning their contingent doubled. As usual, McNeill and Stogsdill were in one car. Sergeant Roy Holland of the AST's Seattle office and Mary Anne Henry were in another. Their destination was a stake out location near Peel's deteriorating house in a neighborhood of modest houses and few pretensions. As John Peel made his way to work, the officers followed him into the parking lot of the Chris Craft boat yard where he was now employed. That was where they stopped him.

The arresting officer was Bellingham detective David McNeill. According to police statements, no guns were drawn. Everybody was trying to stay calm. They got to Peel just as he got out of his truck.

"John Peel," the detective announced as he confronted Peel, "I have a warrant for your arrest on eight counts of murder." As McNeill spoke, Stogsdill dropped back a few feet, then returned to the car. He didn't want even a hint that he was acting improperly. Detective McNeill, meanwhile, started to list the counts against John Peel.

"Count one," he said, his voice clear and strong, "Mark Coulthurst. Count two, Irene Coulthurst. Count three, Kimberly Coulthurst. Count four, John Dease Coulthurst. Count five, Mike Stewart. Count six, Dean Moon. Count seven, Chris Heyman. Count eight, Jerome Keown."

John Peel just stared at him while the charges mounted. "Direct and cold" was the way McNeill described it. And then, according to police statements, John Peel uttered three words.

"Let's do it."

In a later interview for the news magazine *A Current Affair*, John Peel provided his own description of the arrest:

"I was on my way to work and they, ah, pulled up behind me and turned on their sirens, and followed me to the parking lot at work. I just parked in my usual spot at work and they said, 'You're under arrest,' you know.

"The cops came around, about three or four different cop cars, and you know, it looked like they were all ready to draw their guns and stuff, it was pretty frightening, it was pretty embarrassing. There was, you know, a couple hundred people pulling into go to work and, you know, just… Whew… You know, kinda blows you away, you know… And they put the handcuffs on me, and put me in the car and, you know, take me downtown."

After McNeill read Peel his rights, John Peel didn't say another word until they got downtown. When he spoke, it was only to the booking officers when he was being processed into the Whatcom County Jail.

Sergeant Stogsdill slipped further into the background, staying around only long enough to see the booking process begin. Satisfied that his man was going to jail, the trooper made a trip across town. He wanted to talk to Cathy Peel. He wanted John's wife to know he had just been arrested for the *Investor* murders. He didn't want her finding out from some fast-talking reporter chasing a fast breaking story.

Part Two

John Kenneth Peel of Bellingham appeared in Whatcom Superior Court in a ski mask with his attorney, Michael Tario, on Sept. 10, 1984, after his arrest on eight counts of murder. His wife Cathy is behind him on the right, wearing eyeglasses. (Courtesy of the *Bellingham Herald*.)

The *Libby 8*, photographed in Ketchikan, Alaska. Larry Demmert, Jr., Brian Polinkus, Dawn Holmstrom and John Peel worked on this boat during the summer of 1982. (Courtesy of Leland Hale.)

Defense attorney Phillip Weidner (left) and Prosecuting Attorney Mary Ann Henry in Ketchikan Superior Court for pre-trial hearing, August 7, 1985 (Courtesy of Hall Anderson, *Ketchikan Daily News.*)

Sgt. Chuck Miller in the 1970s when he was a Corporal in the Alaska State Troopers. (Courtesy of Col. Tom Anderson, AST, retired.)

Sgt. Jim Stogsdill at the 2014 Soldotna Chamber of Commerce Awards ceremony. (Courtesy of Merrill Sikorski.)

Dean Moon in the 1981 Blaine High School Yearbook. Voted Most Far Out by his classmates, Moon played halfback on the football team and was a champion wrestler, finishing 2nd in Country and 3rd in both District and Regional matches. (Courtesy of Blaine Borderites.)

Jerome Keown in the 1981 Blaine High School Yearbook. Voted Most Dependable by his classmates, he was Class President his Freshman and Senior years at Blaine High and an honor student at Seattle University. (Courtesy of Blaine Borderites.)

14

Ketchikan, Alaska
Friday, February 28 - Saturday, March 1, 1986

February can be the cruelest month in Ketchikan. There's the rain—with about 153 inches of rain per year Ketchikan averages a half-inch a day. Though the rain relents some in February, there's the wind and the cold and the skies that never lose their grey. Even with all that, Ketchikan is a pretty town.

Snug on the shores of Revillagigedo Island, Ketchikan is shoved against the mountains, with scant margin between the narrow coastal plain and the sea. Most of her residents live in homes perched on the steep, thickly forested hills. The flattest part of town is downtown, where many of the buildings were built in the twenties, thirties and early forties. Their plain facades have little ambition to rise above two or three stories, but even the humblest among them seems to have a corner view of the sea.

As pretty as Ketchikan is, it could not overcome the State Office Building, on whose fourth floor John Peel's trial would be held. The SOB, as it is known, is the ugliest building in town. Nothing more than tan slabs of concrete, erected in defiance of any aesthetic save efficiency, it is a place that looks better from the inside. But as the families, press and curious filed in for the first day of *State v. Peel*, its grim face somehow seemed appropriate.

In truth, Peel's attorneys had fought for two years to avoid this moment. They'd been pit bulls in his defense, sending fusillades at every obstacle they encountered, using every lawyerly device imaginable.

Even in their defeats, they made it known they were little inclined to give up or give in.

In Bellingham, attorney Michael Tario had fought the extradition order of Alaska governor Bill Sheffield. They didn't succeed but won two important concessions: the judge ordered that Peel not be photographed during his transfer to Alaska, and officers transporting Peel were further barred from talking to him about the case. John Peel's days of unfettered conversations with state troopers were over.

In Ketchikan, his Alaska attorney, Phillip Weidner, had relentlessly attacked the prosecution's case, pointing to possible "irregularities regarding intimidating witnesses." Grand jury witnesses, he said, had been pushed by troopers into fingering Peel as the suspect in the *Investor* murders. Weidner also accused prosecutors of "economic warfare," in which they were "trying to buy a conviction" with their superior resources of money and manpower.

Those themes also figured into Peel's attempts to raise bail. Peel's family and friends pledged $250,000 and hoped the judge would reduce his bail to that amount. Ketchikan judge Thomas Schulz put bail at a million dollars, bowing to the prosecution argument that he was a flight risk. He didn't think Peel would be able to make that amount, but with the help of friends and family, eventually he did.

With his client free on bail, Weidner had next fought to dismiss the indictment. A reading of court records reveals that the defense motion to dismiss was a scattershot attack on the prosecution case. If you don't dismiss because of the failure to fingerprint the *Investor* skiff, the logic went, maybe you'll dismiss because of the failure to preserve the crime scene, or the lack of timely prosecution, or the failure to present exculpatory evidence.

"Such a course," Weidner concluded, "would be in the best interest of all concerned since Mr. Peel, his attorneys, the Peel family, and other persons connected with the defense, sincerely hope that the true culprit will be pursued and that this senseless and cruel persecution of Mr. Peel will cease."

In an August 30, 1985, conference call, John Peel won his first battle when Judge Schulz dismissed the indictment against him. The judge's decision, however, was based on the narrowest of legal grounds. The prosecution, it seemed, had neglected to tell the grand jury that their arson report found only white gas on the *Investor*. Craig Auto—the sole gas station in town—didn't *sell* white gas. The grand jury had been misled.

It was a small victory disguising a defeat; in dismissing the indictment, Schulz refused to dismiss with prejudice—which would have stopped further prosecution of Peel. After careful consideration, Schulz found no cause for dismissing the murder charges outright. "It's not clear to me the evidence, properly presented, is going to change the result" of a murder and arson indictment against Peel, the judge noted. "Substantial evidence supports holding him for trial."

Prosecuting attorney Mary Anne Henry made a second pass at the grand jury, noting as she did so that, "I don't think it will be long before there will be a second grand jury and Peel will be right back where he was." She was right. On October 4, 1985, John Peel was indicted on eight counts of murder and one count of arson for the second time in twelve months. Once more, Peel's attorneys fought the indictment. This time, they lost—but not without one more battle.

There were extended fights over who was on the jury—Phillip Weidner wanted the "average working man" deciding Peel's guilt or innocence. There were also arguments on what they were to be paid — Weidner wanted jury pay increased from $25 to $100 a day. Ultimately, seventeen people were approved to hear the *Investor* case.

The biggest murder trial in Alaska history could finally begin in the newly refurbished courtroom of the Ketchikan District Court.

No one wanted to be there, least of all the families. The on-again, off-again indictment, the tug-of-war of emotions and bitter words, had taken their toll. "It reminds me of the tide coming in," John Peel's mother, Marilyn, said at one point. "It goes out and you enjoy the sandy beach for a while and then you're overtaken again."

But John Peel's family had rallied behind him. "We're closer now, we have to be," Peel's sister, Kelli Perram, told an interviewer in the months before the trial. "You can't talk to all your friends about this."

That Peel's inner circle of supporters would redouble their efforts and ultimately pledge over a million dollars in property so he could be free on bond indicated how close they had become. At the center of his support system were his two-year-old son, Kenny, and his wife, Cathy. Cathy, said Marilyn Peel, had been "pretty much of a rock." Then she added, "I think if it had been me I would have cried gallons of tears. Maybe she does when she's alone."

Cathy Peel certainly wasn't new to this business. After all, she'd nervously accompanied her husband to one of his earliest interviews with troopers. She was aware of the increased police interest in the months and days before his arrest. She'd talked to Sgt. Stogsdill on the day of John's arrest.

But this case was hard on everyone. The Coulthursts and Moons and Stewarts and Heymans and Keowns had also suffered. Theirs was not a loss that could be overcome by a favorable judge or friendly jury. They had felt anger at the slow march toward justice.

Before the trial, Ruth Moon had called the courtroom atmosphere a "circus" and had decried the "rotten" tactics used by Peel's defense team. "I can't talk to the court," she revealed during the prolonged jury selection process. "If I could, I would say, 'Get on with it.' " Still, she expected a fair trial—and a guilty verdict.

The Coulthursts, meanwhile, felt a double injury. John Peel was a family friend. He'd been to their house, had dated their daughter. Once, they'd made an intoxicated John Peel stay at their house so he wouldn't drive drunk and put his own and other people's lives at risk.

"It's certainly going to be difficult," John Coulthurst had said of the prospect of facing Peel and his family in the courtroom. "We know John so well. We know his family so well. I have no qualms about looking him in the eye," the senior Coulthurst added. "But it's too bad it's made victims of his family, too."

Just thinking of Ketchikan brought back dark memories for the Coulthurst's. On the night of the fire, they'd gotten news that something was amiss on the *Investor*, but weren't particularly alarmed, because they knew the family was on their way home. Sally Coulthurst thought, "Mark's boat's on fire and he doesn't know it yet, but we do."

The bad news arrived at eleven that evening, when they learned there were bodies on Mark's boat. Their phone started to ring incessantly; one of those calls was from the troopers, asking for dental records for everyone on board. From then on, they were on autopilot.

By the next morning, the news of the *Investor* fire had hit the street, and friends and neighbors dropped by to offer condolences. The families of crewmen, meanwhile, were coming by with dental records. That afternoon, John and Sally Coulthurst were on their way to Ketchikan. Already, the news reporters were in their faces.

On the flight north, Sally remembered the last time she'd talked to her son. He had called on the ship-to-shore radio, only days before his birthday and less than a week before the fire. The conversation was difficult, because she had never mastered the art of talking to someone on a ship-to-shore radio. The delays drove her crazy. The break-ups in the transmission caused confusion. But Sally remembered that she had balled Mark out because she hadn't heard from him in a while, and that he'd apologized.

In Ketchikan, the Coulthursts had delivered the dental records but didn't learn much. The troopers told them little, and discouraged them from traveling to Craig. What they did learn was from the newspapers or came second hand.

During their four-day stay in Ketchikan, Sally had consumed massive doses of codeine-laced aspirin. Her headache wouldn't go away. John Coulthurst, meanwhile, lost his treasured gold chain at Ketchikan's Ingersoll Hotel. Everywhere he went for the next few days, he asked people if they'd seen it. He asked in restaurants. He asked in bars. When he asked the Ingersoll bartender about the gold chain, his suspicions grew; the bartender described the chain exactly, down to the ornate Japanese character that hung from its length. John Coulthurst suspected the bartender now had his gold chain. When they returned home to Bellingham, he found the gold chain on his nightstand, where it had been all along.

Judge Schulz, meanwhile, was struggling with the attorneys. He had tried everything to diffuse the tension, but nothing seemed to work. His law clerk, Cammy Oechsli, suggested they get both sides together and have cake and coffee whenever someone had a birthday. So they tried it. They got a birthday cake, but ended up starting a war instead. During fishing season, Schulz even tried to get one attorney from each side to go salmon fishing with him, but couldn't get them in the same boat.

Things got so bad that the attorneys fought over where they were going to sit in the courtroom during trial. Tired of the bickering, Schulz decided who would sit where. No sooner had he decided than the attorneys were back at it, arguing about where John Peel's wife should sit and where the Coulthurst's should sit. Weidner wanted the Peel family to sit in the first row behind the jury box, and Schulz sarcastically suggested, "Hell, why don't we just put Peel and them in the box with the jury?"

The irony in all this was that Schulz had looked forward to the Peel trial. He expected it to be interesting. After all, he reasoned, any case that goes two years before an arrest is bound to present a number of intriguing legal issues. He told his law clerk as much, saying, "This is going to be an interesting trial, because this is not an open and shut case by any stretch of the imagination."

In the end, the judge divided the courtroom like Congress. He didn't want the two sides intermingling. The family of the victims would sit on the same side as the prosecution lawyers. Peel's family would sit behind the defense table.

But the arguing about who would sit where was, to some extent, academic. While John Peel's family—including his wife, mother and father—would move to Ketchikan and spend virtually every day in court, the same could not be said of the victims' families. A combination of factors would prevent the Coulthursts and Moons and the others from keeping a similar full-time commitment. Somehow, they'd have to find money to pay for an extended stay in Ketchikan, because the state wasn't going to do it for them. And a number of them were scheduled to take the witness stand, which precluded them from sitting in court until after they'd testified.

If there was a psychological advantage in this, it went to the defense, because it gave the jury a constant reminder that John Peel did not face them alone.

15

Ketchikan, Alaska
Friday, February 28 - Saturday, March 1, 1986

A fourteen-year veteran of the bench, Superior Court Judge Thomas Schulz was a Westerner through and through. Born in Washington State, reared in Alaska, and educated in Oregon, he had a Westerner's sense of independence and a Westerner's sense of rugged individualism. He had little tolerance for nonsense and was, by his own admission, quick to anger.

Schulz was also a man of deep moral principles, a practicing Catholic who routinely went to Mass. He was a family man, a man who had been married more than twenty years, a man with three children. He saw himself as a conscientious judge; in Ketchikan, he had learned that people knew the difference between someone who'd been smoking pot and someone who'd committed a robbery. They expected Schulz to punish them accordingly.

As the trial began, Schulz's courtroom was packed. He'd switched to the larger of the two Superior Court courtrooms in hopes of accommodating the larger crowds, but it was still cramped. The locals were there to see what an accused mass-murderer really looked like. Some had seen the photos of John Peel in Whatcom County Superior Court, where he wore a brown knit ski mask and a bulletproof vest.[10] Others had learned of his Ketchikan arraignment, when Peel showed up wearing a brown woman's wig, a long brown costume beard and

---

10   "Identity is the only issue of this case as far as I'm concerned," said Peel's attorney, Michael Tario, explaining why his client had worn the ski mask. "I don't want my client's right to a fair trial tainted."

mirrored sunglasses. But the courtroom was bursting at the seams for reasons that went beyond families and curious locals.

Near the jury box was a scale model of the *Investor* and another model of Craig. There, too, were the sketchpads that promised to keep prosecutors busy as they took jurors through the complex maze of facts and circumstance. The exhibits so crowded the courtroom there was scant room for the attorneys to roam.

Leading the prosecution was Mary Anne Henry. 34 years old and single, the Harvard law grad and nine-year veteran of the prosecutor's office was appointed district attorney only two years previous. Just the second woman in Alaska history to hold that position, some described her as a pioneer; Henry insisted she was merely, "the right person at the right time."

She'd cut her teeth in the pipeline-era Anchorage of the mid-seventies, where drugs were sold from hotel windows and the streets were rife with violence. An experienced hand at fast-breaking homicides, there was no soft-pedaling her reputation. She was fiercely competitive, hard working, intelligent and aggressive. Once more, she hoped to be "the right person at the right time."

Henry had every confidence that her case against John Peel was fully loaded. She had an arson investigator ready to testify that the accelerant used on the *Investor* could have contained a mixture of white gas and gasoline. A forensic anthropologist who'd examined the two bags of unidentified bones and found that the remains represented more than one person, thereby accounting for seven of the *Investor's* eight crewmembers. A forensic dentist who compared known x-rays of the victims and determined that some of the specimens came from Chris Heyman. The dentist added that, evidence from what he called "Bag Five," showed "consistencies that would lead me to believe that possibly some of these specimens are from Dean Moon."

If they had Chris Heyman—and if they had Dean Moon—then Johnny Coulthurst was the only one not accounted for. Henry would argue that his body had been totally consumed by the fire. The alternative was too absurd to bear—that four-year-old Johnny Coulthurst was missing because he had shot everyone on board and made a miraculous escape. The layers of defense objections were slipping away like onion skins.

That said, at bottom it was still a circumstantial case, without an obvious "smoking gun." There were dozens of witnesses and, in Henry's estimation, "thousands and thousands and thousands of bits and pieces that are involved." Her task was to build a wall composed of hundreds of bricks; the risk was that the jury would only see the bricks—and never see the wall.

As in any case as complex as the *Investor* murders, however, Henry would not be forced to go it alone.

At her side was Assistant District Attorney Bob Blasco. A 33-year-old University of Maryland Law School graduate, Blasco was known as a good lawyer who vigorously prosecuted the cases before him. If there was a knock on him, it was that he sometimes took his cases too seriously, so much so that local police occasionally found themselves telling him to back off. Henry was also joined at trial by Pat Gullufsen, a former prosecutor who'd been persuaded to temporarily abandon his private practice for the Peel case. Sources close to the prosecution said the Attorney General's office felt they needed Gullufsen's experience and cool head under fire. This trial promised to challenge the prosecution like no other.

On the other side of the courtroom was the defense, which now included Brant McGee with the state's Office of Public Advocacy. McGee, 38, was a Vietnam veteran who'd gone prematurely gray. As one writer described him, McGee looked like a "particularly hip high school guidance counselor." He enjoyed a reputation as a cool, reasonable professional, respected by colleagues and opponents alike.

John Peel, who was sitting next to McGee and only feet from the jury, had an up-close view as Mary Anne Henry began her opening statement and accused him of the crimes. A big-boned woman with plain features, Henry seemed somehow uncomfortable in dresses and heels. As she rose to address the jury for the first time, she scarcely moved. Yet this was one of her most important performances at trial. Although judges tell juries that opening statements are not evidence, jury verdicts are remarkably consistent with the jury's impression of the opening statement.

"This case is about an explosion of human emotion in John Kenneth Peel," Henry proclaimed as the first words left her mouth. "An explosion that triggered him to murder eight people, not by plan, and not by design, but by the simple yet deadly combination of human emotion, anger, frustration, jealousy, humiliation and maybe more—combined with a single event that caused him to fire that first shot. Once he fired that first shot, he had to continue firing shots because everyone on the *Investor* down to John Coulthurst knew John Peel. And when John Peel was done, eight people were dead."

One by one, she named the victims. Mark Coulthurst, 28 years old when he was murdered. Irene Coulthurst, his wife, also 28 years old when she was murdered. Kimberly, their daughter, age five when she was murdered, and Johnny, age four, their son. Dean Moon, nineteen years of age when he was murdered. Jerome Keown, also nineteen when he was murdered. Mike Stewart, Mark Coulthurst's cousin, also nineteen. Chris Heyman, from California, nineteen when he was killed.

In the following ten or fifteen minutes, Henry reeled off more names, in what would become a dizzying list, a list that would challenge even the best memory. Each person held a small part of the big picture and the prosecutor wanted to make sure the jurors knew all the players. By the time she was finished, she had given them 62 people to remember.

Only then did she start to tell the story of the *Investor* and the summer of 1982.

For more than three hours, Mary Anne Henry laid out the evidence that pointed to John Peel. If there was a motive for this crime—and Henry did not mention it explicitly—it was John Peel's burning resentment. John Peel, Henry suggested, had a "lousy season" in 1982. He was stuck on the *Libby 8*, "an old and dirty boat" that "suffered numerous breakdowns." Peel himself estimated that they fished only seven days the entire season. No one was making money; Peel himself made only $4,615 that season. To make matters worse, on the night before the murders, John Peel learned that Dean Moon had just been promoted to skiff operator.

"He was getting twelve percent now," Henry said, speaking of Dean Moon's percentage of the boat's profits, "and they were having a great season. That season John Peel was getting a five percent crew share. That season, Dean Moon made three times what John Peel did. If John Peel was still working for Mark Coulthurst, he'd be working on the

Investor, and he would have been the skiff operator, and he would have gotten twelve percent."

Henry didn't dwell on John Peel's state of mind, however. She told instead of John Peel staggering over the gunnel of the *Investor*. Of a scream heard in the middle of the night. John Peel with a rifle, standing on the dock. John Peel gone missing until the next day. John Peel saying he had been with his girlfriend, when he wasn't. John Peel missing in action again for most of the next two days.

She talked about John Peel taking the boat to Ben's Cove and opening all the valves on the *Investor*. She talked about him taking the *Investor's* skiff and "leaving eight bodies on board what he thought was a sinking ship." She talked about a witness seeing John Peel as he made his way back to Craig. Then she talked about the next day, the day of the fire. She told the jury that the *Investor* hadn't sunk, as John Peel had planned.

"So John Peel went into town and made a phone call at 11:56 a.m. to a travel agency in Ketchikan. John Peel then went to the gas station, Jim Robinson's gas station in Craig, and bought gas, carrying it away in a jerry jug. John Peel took that jerry jug of gasoline and he splashed it all over inside the *Investor*. He saturated those bodies, he poured gasoline in the galley, and then he lit it, jumped back in the skiff and headed straight back to the cold storage dock."

She also told the jury about the people who saw John Peel in the skiff, about the ill-fated attempts to put out the fire, about the discovery of the bodies by Trooper Anderson. She showed them a jerky, out-of-focus film of the *Investor* fire. Mary Anne Henry then described the scene in Bellingham, when John Peel was finally confronted by the police. In Henry's telling, John Peel said everything but the magic words. "John Peel didn't say I didn't do it," Henry said angrily. "John Peel didn't say I'm innocent, man. John Peel didn't even get angry. John Peel started asking questions, trying to find out what the investigators knew."

Weidner objected, interrupting the district attorney in mid-sentence. "Objection," he repeated as Henry kept on talking. "Right to remain silent, and right to counsel, your Honor, it's improper comments."

"Overruled," Judge Schulz replied.

Overruled, but Mary Anne Henry knew she had problems and if she didn't deal with them, Phillip Weidner would deal with them for her. Her biggest problems were Peel's crewmembers on the *Libby 8*. For, while they provided the best evidence against John Peel, they were also very squirrelly. Henry spent the next half hour or so preemptively defending Dawn Holmstrom and Larry Demmert.

These two, Henry said, knew too much. They were afraid, she suggested, and had wanted out of this case. But it was too late. They had already told what they knew, and what they knew implicated John Peel. Still, she suggested, "There is no living person who witnessed those murders, except John Peel. The evidence that you are going to hear will be more than sufficient beyond any reasonable doubt that those emotions came together in John Peel that night and caused him to fire that first shot. The evidence will be clear that John Peel murdered all of those people. And at the end of this case the State will stand before you again and ask you to hold John Peel responsible for what he did."

"The State will ask you to look at John Peel and say, 'John Peel, you murdered Mark Coulthurst.' " Henry glared at Peel as she spoke the words, placing herself at a strategic spot between the prosecution table and the jury. Her voice filled with drama as she forcefully intoned, "John Peel, you murdered Irene Coulthurst; John Peel, you murdered Kimberly and John Coulthurst; John Peel, you murdered Chris Heyman, you murdered Dean Moon, you murdered Mike Stewart, and you murdered Jerome Keown, and then, John Peel, you set them on fire."

"Your Honor, that concludes my opening statement," Henry finally pronounced. "Thank you, ladies and gentlemen, for your time."

Although he could have gone on immediately, defense attorney Phillip Weidner elected not to follow directly on Mary Anne Henry's heels. He wanted to wait until the next morning. He wanted the jury to be "fresh."

16

Ketchikan, Alaska
Friday, February 28 - Saturday, March 1, 1986

Phillip Weidner was added to the defense team because John Peel's Bellingham attorney, Michael Tario, was not a member of the Alaska bar. But Phillip Weidner was no stand-in. John Peel's parents retained him after an intensive search for a skilled attorney capable of beating back the charges against their son.

In the forty-year-old defense specialist, and divorced father of two, they were convinced they had found their man. Their feelings were confirmed when one of his former colleagues told them, "Phil would be like a dog with a bone." His record in murder cases was enviable. Since coming to Alaska, Weidner estimated he had handled thirty murder cases. Of the ten that went to trial, only one resulted in a conviction—and was on appeal at the time of the Peel trial.

Born on a tenant farm in the hill country of southern Illinois in 1946, Weidner still remembered shucking corn by hand. Yet whatever else he was, Phillip Paul Weidner was no hayseed. His undergraduate degree was from the prestigious Massachusetts Institute of Technology. His law degree was taken from Harvard Law in 1972. Like many of his contemporaries, the Vietnam War radicalized him. During the 1968 Democratic convention, Weidner spent a few days getting tear-gassed by the Chicago police.

As an attorney, he dedicated his practice to working for personal rights against state authority and power. "I take my oath as an attorney seriously," he once said. "For me that means representation of the downtrodden."

He was an unmistakable presence in the courtroom, with his long hair, flowing beard and penchant for long coats and rope belts. At its best, his voice was soft and hypnotic, although his word-flow sometimes bordered on the apoplectic. As he began his opening statement the day following Mary Anne Henry's presentation, Weidner shelved the bombast. He was at pains to gain the sympathy of the jury. They were in this together, as "good and humble people." He didn't hesitate to tell of his own humble background in Illinois, implying that he was a backwoods lawyer cut from the same cloth as Abraham Lincoln.

"Ladies and gentlemen of the jury, good people of Ketchikan," he said as he began his defense of John Peel, "we come now to commit your hearts and your minds and your conscience to the life of John Kenneth Peel, the citizen accused in this case. We come now to show why you must join with us in stopping this terrible mistake. Why this rush to judgment—and the evidence will show that this is a rush to judgment—why this attempt to construct a solution to an admittedly terrible crime at any cost?"

"Now Ms. Henry, skilled prosecutor that she is," Weidner continued, "is seeking this conviction, this rush to judgment. She's told a terrible story. A carefully, artfully constructed illusion of terror. A balloon puffed up with fear. One that I know must have struck some fear into your hearts. I noticed yesterday that some of you appeared to be on the verge of tears, maybe crying. And it must have brought some chill to your soul. And I'm sure that maybe when you heard that story, you may have had some fear about John Peel. Maybe the stirrings of anger or hate may have started."

"The evidence will show that the prosecution in this case, they've adopted basically a see-no reality, hear-no reality, speak-no reality approach to this case," Weidner insisted. What the prosecution had missed, according to Weidner, was the true nature of the crime. The *Investor* murders, he suggested, were "totally consistent with a professional killing."

"And I'm just talking about circumstantial evidence here. That this evidence is totally consistent with a professional killer. The evidence will show that the real killer, not John Kenneth Peel, but the real person that set that boat on fire, coolly, audaciously, in front of that whole town, set that boat on fire, drove back, got out of that skiff and disappeared into thin air. That's the mark of a professional killer. He doesn't care about being seen. He's never going to be seen again. The shots themselves, the .22 shots in the head—a terrible thing to talk about, but the mark of a professional killer."

After his almost nonchalant suggestion that the murders were the result of organized crime figures operating in the remote fishing village of Craig, Alaska, the defense attorney returned to a theme he had raised often since John Peel's arrest. That theme was prosecutorial misconduct, although Weidner didn't put it that way when he addressed the jury.

Instead, he told them that the prosecution had manipulated witnesses into telling stories that fit their theory of the case. He pointed to the immunity several witnesses received to protect them from statements they had made to the first grand jury, statements they'd had second thoughts about, statements that Weidner said were lies. One of the witnesses took the Fifth Amendment "97 times," he told them, because "it might incriminate him to answer questions."

Phillip Weidner also spoke of drug deals and suggested that a former *Libby 8* crewmember had come to Craig "to sell cocaine." He mentioned a host of other suspects and possible explanations—a man who had allegedly "cased" the *Investor* to commit a robbery; the possibility that someone wanted to kill Mark Coulthurst because he had "rammed a Native boat over in Craig;" the "informants" who suggested the Coulthurst's were killed because Mark "was dealing in kilos of cocaine;"[11] and finally there was Dean Moon, who may have been responsible because, "I don't know if Dean Moon is dead or not."

But whoever did it, he suggested, it wasn't John Peel, because John Peel lacked a motive. John Peel and Mark Coulthurst, Weidner explained, "had a mutual parting of the ways." In his first direct attack on the police, Weidner also suggested that, "there is missing evidence in this case." Like the gas can that had been in the *Investor* skiff. Or

---

11   The focus on cocaine was in keeping with the times. Federal drug surveys show that cocaine use peaked in the United States in 1982 at 10.4 million users. It was seen as a glamorous drug, associated with the work-hard party-hard lifestyle of the 1980s—and those who aspired it. The drug was also inextricably associated with the hyper-violent Colombian cartels, with trade routes north to Miami and California.

the failure to fingerprint anything but the nozzle on that gas can and a length of tie line.

To the other lawyers in the room, this was territory he'd already traversed in his many attacks against the indictment. But now, for the first time in years, he had a fresh audience. This time around, the court was in no position to contradict him.

By the time Phillip Weidner reached the end of his opening statement, he had referenced Thomas Jefferson.

"He was defending a man charged in the Boston Massacre," Weidner said. "He was defending an English soldier who had been a bystander, but someone claimed that somehow he had fired the shot that started it." And he talked to the jury, saying, "I've read that address. And he said, ladies and gentlemen, when you decide the fate of this young soldier, treat him like you would if he was an American being tried in England."

"And that's what I say to you now. John Peel is from Bellingham. Can you imagine what it would be like for a boy from Ketchikan to be down in Bellingham right now and being falsely accused and tried for a murder he didn't commit? And to be looking at sixteen people from Bellingham and wondering will they be fair, will they insist on real proof, will they follow the law? We, we don't wonder, because we know you will. You're going to do what's right, and you're going to bring back a not guilty verdict, and I'm going to thank you for that."

With those words, Phillip Weidner was nearly finished. Although it had taken the better part of two days, both sides had been given their say. After all the talking and all the speechmaking, the trial could finally begin.

17

Ketchikan, Alaska – Craig, Alaska
Monday, March 3, 1986

This was the morning when the jurors, Judge Schulz, and John Peel—along with the defense attorneys, the prosecutors, investigators, court bailiffs and several reporters—were stuck at the Ketchikan seaplane dock, waiting for the fog to lift. No one was really supposed to say much beyond "small talk," and they all knew about the weather. In the small world that's "Alaska," that could qualify as claustrophobic.

Several hours passed before they clambered on board one of the four float planes, bound for Craig, sixty or so miles due west.

Once airborne, they endured a bumpy ride. Buffeted by gusty winds, the four de Havilland Beavers dipped and bobbed, seeming to pause in midair before gathering themselves and surging onward. Below them passed Gravina Island, followed by the churning waters of Clarence Strait, then the dark-green forests that clogged Prince of Wales Island, relieved only by random patches of clear-cut timber. If they were lucky, they recognized Skowl Arm and Old Frank's Lake. Otherwise, they clung to their toothbrushes and extra socks, packed in case the weather grounded them in Craig.

They landed to a driving rain that drenched the landscape in sheets of grey. From the Craig seaplane base, the bailiffs shuffled the jurors into two waiting vans; the remainder of the party followed in a third, driven by Judge Schulz. They took a left turn along Water Street and made the short drive to North Cove dock, where John Peel was accused of killing the *Investor* captain and his crew. Barren in the off-season, they had to imagine the fishing boats crammed edge-to-edge as they made the long trek to the end of the dock, where the *Investor*, and the *Libby 8*, had been moored the night of the murders.

The jurors barely lingered. The next item on their itinerary was an Alaska Department of Fish and Game boat; after donning life preservers, many of them flown in with them from Ketchikan to ensure that everyone had a life jacket, they headed out to Ben's Cove on Fish Egg Island, a mile and a half north of Craig. It was there that the killer first attempted to sink, and ultimately torched, the *Investor* in a desperate bid to cover up the crime.

From the protected waters of the cove, Craig was no longer visible. Nor were the remains of the *Investor*. The jurors had to imagine the blaze that stubbornly refused to extinguish, had to conjure the bodies languishing on board, unbeknownst to firefighters. In the courtroom, the prosecution would show them a model of the *Investor*, but it was only that. A model.

The *Investor* itself was resting at the bottom of a bay six miles to the southeast. It had sunk as it was being towed to the Lower 48 for refitting, having been sold by the Coulthurst estate to new owners. Peel's attorney's had asked Judge Schultz to order it to be refloated. Because of its loss, they complained, "the defense is now in the posture of having to search the bottom of the ocean for the scene of the alleged crime."

Though sympathetic, Schulz had turned them down and, in the instant case, he had other worries. Weeks earlier, while he and the attorneys were in town to establish the ground rules of the visit, he had been admonished by a Craig police officer for speeding. He was now determined to drive cautiously.

After lunch, the jurors were taken on a walking tour of Craig. They visited the cannery dock, where the killer ditched the *Investor* skiff after setting the seine boat on fire. Then they trekked several different routes to the First Bank branch on Main Street. It was a detail that was sure to arise during the course of the trial.

John Peel maintained that he'd encountered crewmate Dawn Holmstrom as she walked from the dock to the bank in the moments after the *Investor* was set ablaze. They were, as the defense story went, together when the smoke of the fire was first sighted. Bingo. John Peel could not have torched the *Investor*.

Whether the defense theory was credible, however, depended on the timing of two critical events. The first of these was the timing of the mayday calls *Casino* skipper Bruce Anderson made to the Coast Guard. The second was the timing of a phone call Peel made from Craig that same evening, the proof of which came courtesy of the State Troopers.

The first recorded call on the Coast Guard transcript was made at 4:34 p.m. John Peel's phone call had been made at 4:59 p.m. In those scant 25 minutes, John Peel, having already torched the boat, would have had to take the skiff toward Craig, speak briefly with the *Casino* crew, land at the cold storage dock, make his way to Craig—which by police estimates took at least ten minutes—then meet with Dawn Holmstrom before finally making the phone call. Such a scenario, the defense suggested, was impossible.

But was the 4:34 p.m. call the first mayday? Mary Anne Henry contended that it wasn't. An examination of the Coast Guard log revealed that the 4:34 p.m. call had been made from Ben's Cove—not from the cold storage dock where Bruce Anderson called in his first mayday. According to the Coast Guard transcript, 4:34 p.m. was the time when the "*Casino rpts the Investor engulfed in flames. Can see no one on board or in water.*"

That language was consistent only with a report from the fire scene, and Bruce Anderson had testified at the second grand jury that he had seen the *Investor* fire and broadcast at least two maydays before 4:34 p.m. It was the prosecution's view that that there was more than enough time for the accused to talk to the *Casino* crew on the way to town, ditch the skiff and meet Dawn Holmstrom in Craig. From there it was short jaunt to the Hill Bar, where telephone records showed that John Peel called home.

What jurors didn't see that day—what they couldn't see—was the Craig that had hosted the *Investor* murders. Not only was it the off-season now, but Craig was changing, with a new jail and a professionalized police force. In 1982, Craig was a village with minimal police presence and a rough reputation. As one long-time resident told a visiting reporter, "Craig has always been wild. And there's no getting over that."

Back then there were only two cops, no jail and one Alaska State trooper for the entire island. Sometimes called "Little Chicago," alcohol-driven fights were common in Craig. There were stories about guys getting beat up and guys getting stabbed. Sometimes the fights turned into brawls. Sometimes firearms were involved. Back in the day, murders were an inconvenience, more likely to be ignored than punished.

When the fish were running, the harbor was jammed with fishing boats; the cannery was running at full speed; Craig's population nearly doubled with transient workers and fishermen. Guys, young guys, who had been cooped up for months were looking for ways to spend their hard-earned pay. In villages like Craig, the movie theater ran one show a week. After they'd seen the movie, there was nothing to do but drink or go crazy or both. With three bars, Craig was well positioned to serve them all the booze and crazy they could handle.

Now that the fishermen were gone, Craig turned bucolic. Local kids took fishing boats to basketball games, there being no other form of transportation between some of the villages. The town was so safe, no one bothered to lock their doors.

The only part of Craig's wild side that juror's saw was a pack of dogs that confronted them before running off. In Craig, the average dog was the size of a wolf.

18

No battle was more important than that for the souls of John Peel's crewmates on the *Libby 8*. Their words, more than any other's, could help close the door on John Peel's guilt. Their words could just as surely set him free. None of them loomed larger than Larry Demmert, Jr.

As far back as Craig, in the days after the murders, Larry Demmert had hinted that he knew more than he was willing to tell. It took him two years to finally spring it free.

The first hint came when Trooper Anderson and the Craig police chief interviewed him at the *Libby 8*, on the day after the fire. Demmert was cold and uncommunicative, saying only that, "I haven't seen John in a couple of days." The Craig police chief, who had known Larry Demmert since they were kids, sensed there was more to it than that; he sensed that the skipper was being less than cooperative.

"Mr. Demmert knows more than he's saying," he whispered to Anderson at the time. "I know Larry Demmert."

In November 1983, Demmert provided a glimpse into that "something more." On the night before the murders, he calmly told Stogsdill, he saw someone on the dock who appeared to match the skiffman's description. But, he added, he had never seen that person before. He also told the sergeant he remembered waking up at 2:00 a.m. Monday morning. He said it was for a "funny reason." He didn't think anyone else was aboard the *Libby 8*, because he didn't hear any sounds.

This was the second time Demmert had spoken of awakening that Monday morning. Only months earlier, he called the Bellingham police and told them of waking up to "something strange."

"I felt evil," Demmert had asserted. "I felt evil in the air."

In early '84, the Larry Demmert show got even more curious. Asked to bring some of his ammunition to the police station, Demmert told Bellingham detective Dave McNeill to meet him at the Clark Market on James Street. He didn't want the cop coming near his home, because he was scared and afraid someone might be watching his house. In March, Peel's skipper told them that, as he returned to *Libby 8* on the evening of the murders, he saw someone clambering onto the *Investor*.

Then, on the day of Peel's arrest, Demmert came into the Bellingham Police Department to tell Stogsdill that John's brother, Robert Peel, had fished with him during the 1984 season in Alaska. Demmert claimed that Robert Peel told him his brother would begin to cry whenever he talked about the *Investor*.

By the time of the first grand jury in September of 1984, Larry Demmert was reeling from the stress of what he knew. As the Bellingham witnesses flew in from Seattle on the 18th of that month, Dave McNeill noticed that the *Libby 8* skipper had a drink in his hand. Although it seemed a little early to begin drinking, that wasn't the problem. The problem was that Larry Demmert didn't drink. Before they landed, McNeill learned something else. While Demmert was in the restroom, his seatmates told him Demmert wasn't drinking.

"He's eating Valium," they said.

The following morning, Demmert was standing near the elevator in the State Office Building, just down the hall from Mary Anne Henry's office. Dawn Holmstrom called Detective McNeill over and told him that Demmert was "acting strange." She said, "He's packing a gun around town."

Catching Demmert in the hallway, the troopers hustled him into Mary Anne Henry's office. Once there, Stogsdill didn't mince words. "I want that gun," he told Demmert.

"Well, okay," Demmert replied. He immediately handed over the weapon, which, Stogsdill discovered, was a .357. Court documents indicate that Stogsdill immediately unloaded it, put the bullets in his pocket and placed the gun in Mary Anne Henry's desk drawer. She locked it after him. Then they led the *Libby 8* skipper to a conference room next to Henry's office. They wanted to find out what the hell was going on.

"Why are you carrying a gun?" Stogsdill had demanded once the door was closed.

Demmert gave him a long, rambling explanation. He told them he was scared. He told them he was afraid to walk down the street without carrying a gun. Somebody might recognize him, Demmert said, because he had a lot of relatives in Ketchikan and was known in the area. With a gun he felt safer. At least he could defend himself.

"Why are you scared?" Stogsdill asked.

"Because I'm a star witness in this case," Demmert told him. "Me and Dawn are important witnesses in this case."

Demmert's response surprised the trooper. "Well, frankly, what you've had to say up to this point is important, Larry," Stogsdill told him. "But you know, if something were to happen to you this afternoon, the case would still go on without you."

Demmert seized his opportunity. He told the trooper he didn't want to testify. He was afraid to testify and did not want to be involved in the case. For one thing, he told them, he had never been involved in a case like this before. He added that, the person he would have to testify against—John Peel—was a very close friend of his. He was scared, he said, and what he was afraid of was retaliation. John Peel, he told him, had friends everywhere.

"Normal people don't want to testify against their friends," Stogsdill assured him. "But sometimes they have to…"

To put his mind at ease, Stogsdill had pulled out one of John Peel's statements, one in which Peel implicated Demmert in the *Investor* murders. Demmert was surprised, but didn't get angry. Instead, he started asking questions about perjury. What was it? If he said one thing in one statement and another thing in a different statement—was that perjury? Stogsdill patiently explained that, based on the examples he'd given them, Demmert hadn't committed perjury.

"You commit perjury," he told him, "when you go before a judicial body and purposely lie. And as far as I'm concerned, up to this point you haven't done that."

But Demmert was concerned enough that he'd called the fishermen's association and had them send him an attorney. After speaking to the attorney, Demmert calmed down considerably. Calmed down enough that Stogsdill made him an offer. He would return his gun if he promised to put it in the hotel safe and leave it there until he left town. Demmert agreed to the offer.

The next day, McNeill, Blasco and trooper Roy Holland worked with Larry Demmert to make sure he was ready to face the grand jurors. Demmert quickly took them through the sequence of events, as if he just wanted to get it over with. But McNeill insisted that he start over again, from the top. That's when things got interesting.

After telling his "audience" what they already knew—that he had returned to the *Libby 8* sometime between ten and eleven on Sunday evening, that he had seen someone on the boat next to the *Investor* and observed that person going onto the deck of the *Investor*—he told them something they had never heard before. He told them that the person he saw that night was "John." Just the sound of the words coming from his mouth made him emotional. The court record notes that Demmert started to shake. The tears started pouring from his eyes.

"John who?" Detective McNeill asked.

"John Peel," Demmert replied, his voice quavering, the tears now flowing freely.

"Why do you think it was John Peel?" the detective asked.

Larry Demmert struggled to speak. In between sobs, he said he had known John Peel most of his life. He added that the way the person was moving onto the boat, plus his silhouette and physical characteristics, immediately brought John Peel to mind. Given the gravity of what Demmert had just revealed, the detective wanted Larry Demmert to start over again, from the beginning, from the time he first hit the dock. Satisfied that Demmert's story was consistent in the re-telling, McNeill then asked, "What happened next?"

"I got on board the *Libby 8*," he replied, adding that it was tied up next to his dad's boat, the *Cindy Sue*. The *Investor*, he said, was only a short distance away. And, he said, he believed he was the only person on board the "*8*."

"And then what happened?" McNeill wanted to know.

Larry Demmert forced out the words, seeming to pause between each phrase. "I slept for a while," he told them. "And then I woke up at about 2:00 a.m. I don't know why I think it's 2:00 a.m. But that's what time I think it was. And I woke up suddenly. I heard some noises. Like 'pop, pop, pop, pop.' It sounded like backfires from a small engine. And then I heard the scream of a woman."

Larry Demmert started shaking again. Once more, his eyes filled with tears. He could barely speak.

"What kind of scream was it?" McNeill asked him. "What did it sound like?"

Between sobs, Demmert had told them it was a "blood-curdling scream. It sounded like somebody was getting murdered." Larry Demmert broke down again, and then recovered enough to reveal additional information. "I looked out the porthole and looked outside," he noted. "Everything seemed quiet and motionless. I had an eerie feeling about the situation. And I was extremely scared."

"So what did you do?" McNeill wondered.

"I sat there for a few minutes. Then I opened up my cabin door. And when I looked out, I saw someone walking across the other boats. And the first thing I noticed was this guy had a blue baseball cap with a gold marijuana leaf on it. And then I noticed it was John Peel."

"What was he doing?"

"In his right hand, he was carrying a rifle, with the gun barrel pointed in an upwards fashion. And it was fairly close to his body. And that really scared me," he admitted. "I saw John Peel and I thought about the gun and the noise I'd heard and the scream..."

"What was he wearing?" McNeill inquired. "Tell me what he was wearing."

"A plaid colored shirt or jacket," Demmert replied, becoming increasingly upset. "And the blue baseball cap with the marijuana leaf."

Larry Demmert now broke down completely. His body shaking with emotion, he put his head in his hands and lowered it to the table. "Oh, God," he moaned as he was overtaken by convulsive sobs. He started blubbering uncontrollably and Sergeant Holland brought him Kleenex.

"Just take your time, Larry," Detective McNeill told him. "Just take your time."

Not sure what would help, they brought him a cup of coffee. Demmert tried to take a drink, but he was shaking too much. He finally managed a sip, but something started him crying again and, quivering with pain, he lost control of his body and started to vomit.

That time, it took quite a while for Larry Demmert to recover. All McNeill, Holland and Blasco could do was wait. Their patience was rewarded when Demmert finally gathered enough strength to tell them what happened next. "I closed the door to my stateroom," he told them, "and was listening." What he heard was a "thump" on the deck of his boat, which told him someone was coming on board. Still frightened by what he had seen and heard, Demmert told them he reached over and locked his cabin door. Then he lay down on the bunk, covered himself up with a blanket and hid.

While he was hiding, Demmert said, he heard the footsteps of someone going into the fo'c's'le of the *Libby 8*. Moments later, he heard the footsteps again, this time going onto the deck and off the boat.

"What were you feeling?" McNeill asked.

"I was extremely frightened," Demmert revealed. "I was afraid for my life."

So frightened that he had trouble falling asleep. So frightened that he was restless and woke up again at six in the morning. When he looked out the porthole of the "8," he saw the *Investor* drifting away from the dock. Saw someone in the wheelhouse. Someone wearing a baseball cap. Again, Demmert was overcome by his emotions. McNeill wanted to know why.

"I wondered what my crewman was doing in the wheelhouse," Demmert explained. The person in the wheelhouse was looking straight at him. Demmert said it scared him. He said he "didn't want to die," and revealed that the person he saw was John Peel. "At least I think it was John," Demmert added, revealing that the lighting was "somewhat dim."

"I'm not positive," he continued, "but I'm pretty sure it was John."

19

Ketchikan, Alaska
Thursday, March 6, 1986

L arry Demmert, Jr., was important enough that the prosecution saw fit to prepare him for the expected onslaught by Phillip Weidner. In the months before the trial, he met with Sergeant Stogsdill at Demmert's attorney's office in Seattle. He met a second time with Stogsdill in Bellingham. He also met several times with Stogsdill and assistant district attorney Bob Blasco at pre-trial meetings in Ketchikan. They had talked to him, in Stogsdill's words, "about being in court, what it was like."

Larry Demmert's testimony was also important enough that Mary Anne Henry was willing to risk granting him immunity for his trial testimony, to protect him from discrepancies in his grand jury statements that exposed him to perjury. Henry later admitted that the grant of immunity had scared her, because it gave Demmert "an easy out." He could have said that he was John Peel's skipper, she noted, and then copped out by saying, "he's a nice guy and that's all I can tell you."

On the witness stand, Larry Demmert looked vulnerable, his raven-colored hair slinking to his shoulders, his eyes blinking nervously. Speaking softly, sometimes emotionally, he didn't retreat into immunity, as Henry had feared he might. Demmert affirmed most of his earlier testimony.

Under questioning by assistant district attorney Bob Blasco, he stood by his statement that he had seen a drunken John Peel clambering aboard the *Investor* on the night of the murders. He stood by the statement that he had seen John Peel on a North Cove dock with what looked like a rifle in his hand. The only statement he now doubted was the one he made before the first grand jury, when he said he saw John Peel in the wheelhouse of the *Investor* the following morning.

Larry Demmert's most emotional moment came when he described what he felt when he suddenly awakened on the night of the murders. "When I woke up I was real scared," he said. "Never been that scared in my life. I don't know why. It was like there was a danger in the air or evil in the air. It was just real thick. I had like goose pimples, felt like I was just… for some reason, my nerves were all on end."

John Peel was expressionless as he watched his friend testify, moving only to occasionally scribble notes in a yellow legal pad. He did not squirm when he heard Demmert say he had looked out his stateroom window after hearing the scream. He did not flinch when his former skipper said he saw "John Peel standing on the dock. Looked like he may have had a rifle in his hand." He was emotionless when Demmert added that he recognized him, in part, because Peel was wearing his "town hat."[12]

As the day's testimony continued, Demmert added other circumstantial details. He said he found his H&R .22 caliber pistol in the wheelhouse of the *Libby 8*, which struck him as unusual because, "I usually kept it down in the stateroom." He said John Peel spent little time at the boat during the next two days and that, at one point, he sent Brian Polinkus after him.

"And about twenty minutes later Brian didn't show up," Demmert said. "I went up and found them both at the Hill Bar. I told them to get their butts down to the boat." Peel only stayed at the boat for ten or fifteen minutes, the *Libby 8* skipper said, before he took off again.

Demmert told the jury that the next time he saw John Peel was the day of the fire, after his first trip to the scene on the *Cindy Sue*. Peel was standing on the cannery dock. He "appeared to be breathing a little heavy," Demmert said. His face was flushed and "a little red." His hair was "messed up." The skipper asked his crewman if he wanted to go out to the fire on the *Cindy Sue*. "He said I don't want to go and watch them

---

12   One of the hazards of seine fishing in Alaska is the jellyfish that tumble out of the nets along with the salmon. Their sting can be debilitating, so most fishermen wear a baseball cap for protection. These hats get slimed by the jellyfish and are not suitable for wearing in town. Hence, the "town hat," which is pristine by comparison and never used on the fishing grounds.

burn," Demmert testified. "I'm not real sure if he said, 'm' as in 'them,' or 'it.' I think it was an 'm.' It struck me very strange."

Knowing his drug use would become an issue, Blasco asked Demmert why he started taking Valium. The skipper explained that he was prompted to get a prescription for the muscle relaxer when troopers started asking him questions about John Peel in March of 1984. He blamed his increasing drug dependence on the "stress, fear and emotion" associated with suspicions his friend had killed the *Investor* crew.

"I didn't want to testify against a friend," he said. He was so afraid that he bought a .375 magnum handgun, "for my own protection."

Blasco also asked Larry Demmert, Jr., why he had withheld information from the State Troopers. The skipper replied that he "didn't want to be involved in the case" and besides, he was a friend of John Peel's. "I grew up with the attitude that you don't talk to the cops," he added. "You don't rat on a friend."

Demmert went on to say that he had purposefully downplayed his testimony before both grand juries, hoping to make himself less valuable at trial. That explained why he had told the grand jury he might have been awakened by a dream, not a scream. That explained why he had said he wasn't sure he saw a rifle in John Peel's hand.

"I was trying to soften up my testimony," Demmert told Blasco. "It was an easier way out. I tried to make it seem as if my testimony wasn't critical, I guess."

By midday, Demmert had acknowledged a number of subtle—and not so subtle—changes he'd made in his testimony. Faced with those changes, Blasco wondered aloud if the *Libby 8* skipper was finally satisfied with his statements. Yes, John Peel's friend told him. He had made all the changes he was going to make. He had only changed them as much as he needed to make the truth known. Now all Larry Demmert had to do was face the defense.

20

Ketchikan, Alaska
Monday, March 10, 1986

The prosecution knew Phillip Weidner was going after Larry Demmert, Jr. They just didn't know where he'd hit him. There seemed to be a wealth of choices and the state's careful handling of Demmert tried to anticipate them all. But a three-day weekend had passed since John Peel's skipper had been on the stand. Weidner would doubtless study the skipper's testimony and pick it apart, looking for some new way to attack.

In fact, court documents reveal that Phillip Weidner had already interviewed Larry Demmert and questioned him intensely about his recollections on the night of the murders. He'd wanted to ask Demmert about mistakes in his grand jury testimony, mistakes he'd shared with John Peel's sister, Kelli Perram. Weidner even brought Perram with him, along with co-counsel Brant McGee and a defense investigator.

In those interviews, conducted before the trial, he'd gotten Demmert to admit he wasn't positive about the identity of the shadowy figure he'd seen in the *Investor* wheelhouse. Weidner pushed that line of reasoning to Larry Demmert's other memories, but Demmert was unshakable in his insistence that he had seen John Peel on the night of the murders, coming off the *Investor*, with what looked like a rifle barrel.

"During that time now," Weidner had interjected, "was that also kind of a shadowy figure situation when he came off and..."

"Oh, there was lights on the boat," Demmert replied. "I recognized him there."

"Is it possible that that was just somebody that kind of looked like Peel, too?"

"No," Demmert replied. "I mean that's—he was twenty feet away." Later in the same conversation, Demmert insisted, "That's the only real positive time that I can positively ID John Peel, was that time."

Larry Demmert Jr. was so unshakable that, at trial, Weidner was forced to try another tactic, one that the crafty defense attorney had also explored during the pre-trial interview of Larry Demmert.

"Good afternoon, Mr. Demmert," Phillip Weidner said as he stood and faced Larry Demmert in the courtroom.

"Good afternoon," Demmert replied.

"Mr. Demmert," Weidner continued, "you are a drug addict, are you not?"

Bob Blasco shot out of his seat. "I'll object, Your Honor," he said, outraged at Weidner's audacity.

"It's relevant, Your Honor," Weidner protested.

"He's arguing with the witness," Blasco responded. "There's no foundation for that."

"I'll sustain the objection," Schulz replied.

"Are you a drug addict?" Weidner asked, rephrasing the question.

"I'll object again, Your Honor," Blasco said.

"Again, I'll sustain the objection," Schulz responded.

"Are you addicted to drugs?" Weidner asked, playing variations on a theme.

"Your Honor," Blasco sighed with exasperation, "I'm going to object and I'll ask to approach the bench."

The judge didn't need a bench conference to make his ruling. He had already let it be known where he stood on questions about drugs. In case anyone had forgotten, he wanted to remind them. "I just want to state that on at least one occasion, I think a couple, I had ruled that addiction generally is irrelevant," the judge said sternly. "I will allow all the inquiry that's necessary into specific drug usage at the times the witness has testified to the events he has testified to, but not beyond that. The objection is sustained."[13]

---

13 Weidner's addiction argument relied heavily on cases dealing with government informers who were addicted to heroin and, for that reason, were particularly susceptible to government pressure. Larry Demmert was not a government informer, was not involved in heroin specifically or narcotics generally, and was

The objection was sustained, but the damage was done. The suggestion, once made, could not be magically withdrawn. Nor was Weidner playing the riverboat gambler, trying to bluff his way through a weak hand. Larry Demmert, Jr., had himself said he was addicted to drugs when he testified before the first grand jury. After hearing three objections sustained, the defense attorney immediately confronted the skipper with his past statements about drug use.

Demmert did his best to hedge. Yes, he admitted, he had told the first grand jury he was addicted to Valium. What he meant by that was merely that he had "little control over the amount or frequency of taking Valium." Demmert insisted that he didn't have any medical evidence of addiction and that his addiction was entirely mental.

"So this was an addiction you could stop and start?"

"That's why I don't know if I was addicted or not," Demmert replied.

Weidner kept after Demmert about his drug use, often skirting dangerously close to the limits set by the judge. On at least one occasion, he stepped over the line. As his cross-examination proceeded, Weidner started reading a particularly long passage about Demmert's drug use, taken from his grand jury testimony. Bob Blasco held his tongue until Weidner neared a portion of that document which was clearly out of bounds. Before the defense could recite the words, Blasco objected.

After a bench conference, Judge Schulz forbade Weidner from reading the offending passage. But the attorney cleverly stuck in a bit of it anyway. After announcing that he had been precluded from mentioning that part of Demmert's testimony, Weidner noted that the statement included, "some general talk about whether or not you used drugs." The judge was not amused.

"Now look," Schulz commanded from the bench. "When I make a ruling excluding some evidence, we don't have to tell everybody what it was all about."

"I did not mean to..." Weidner insisted.

---

not charged with violating narcotics laws. That said, there is a notion in American jurisprudence that these things matter, as noted in 81 Am. Jur. 2d re: *Witnesses* (1976): "In determining the credibility of a witness, and the weight accorded his testimony, regard may be had to his age and mental or physical condition, such as whether the witness is a child, is intoxicated, is a narcotics addict, or is insane or of unsound and feeble mind."

"That's the reason for the exclusion," Schulz continued. "Don't do it again."

But Larry Demmert's drug use wasn't the only topic of the day. Weidner pounded him for pleading the Fifth Amendment and asking for immunity. Once again, he tried to leave the impression that Demmert took the Fifth because he was lying. Demmert countered that he pled the Fifth Amendment to get his "immunity hearing in front of the Court." Weidner further attacked Demmert for his multiple meetings with prosecutors, suggesting they were "telling you what they expected your testimony to be."

Before the day was over, Weidner also attacked Demmert for his identification of John Peel. In his trial testimony, Demmert said he wasn't sure what his crewman was wearing that night. At the first grand jury, however, Demmert had sworn Peel was wearing a flannel shirt. Weidner tried to make the most of Demmert's apparent about-face. "Since you were trying to convince someone you had seen John Peel," he said accusingly, "you thought you'd throw in the flannel shirt, isn't that true?"

Demmert denied the accusation. Weidner continued to press the question, wondering aloud if the skipper had testified about the flannel shirt just because he thought that's what Peel would have been wearing. But he didn't leave it at that.

"Did you see the person's face?" Weidner asked.

"No, I did not," Demmert replied.

"You didn't see a face at all?" Weidner asked incredulously. "You didn't see a face at all as to anyone going onto the *Investor*?"

"The face?" Demmert said. "No."

"So you're making an identification of a person based upon a view that you can't see their face and maybe you can see something that looks like the hood of a sweatshirt?"

"No," Demmert insisted. "Just by the person's size and shape, the person. The way the person—just the way the person looked."

"And what was the size, how tall?"

"To me, it looked like John Peel," Demmert said.

Weidner tried to shake Larry Demmert, Jr. He asked him if he thought John Peel had such a distinctive height that it distinguished him from the "general male population of Craig or Ketchikan."

Demmert said, "No."

He asked him if he thought John Peel had such a distinctive build that it was "much different than the general population of Craig or Ketchikan."

Demmert again said, "No." Weidner asked him if he thought the shape of John Peel's head was different.

"I recognized him," Demmert said stubbornly. "The thought came to my mind that it was John Peel."

After questioning Demmert for a half day, the defense attorney finally relented. Larry Demmert was able to step down from the stand—at least for the rest of the day. He hadn't buckled under Weidner's withering cross-examination, although Weidner had managed to take some of the gloss out of his statements.

Still, the prosecution had reason to be optimistic. Larry Demmert had known John Peel for nearly two decades. He had spent the entire summer working next to him. Under Weidner's questioning, he had revealed that he was standing only "twenty to thirty feet" away from John Peel when he saw him struggling over the rail of the *Investor*. Even Weidner knew that was far from Demmert's most definitive identification of John Peel.

But Phillip Weidner wasn't finished. For the next several days, he assailed Larry Demmert mercilessly. If there was one comfort for Larry Demmert it was that, courtesy of the Fisherman's Association, he had his own attorney in the courtroom to protect him. That fact notwithstanding, Weidner hit hard on his twin themes of drug addiction and police intimidation. He cunningly referred to Demmert's pre-grand jury interview as an "interrogation." Images of bright lights and snarling detectives came to mind. When he noticed that Larry was continually blinking his eyes, Weidner called attention to it, asking if there was a reason why he kept blinking.

By midday of Demmert's third day of cross-examination, the prosecution had finally heard enough. They requested a hearing before Judge Schulz, seeking a remedy to what Mary Anne Henry characterized as Phillip Weidner's "misconduct."

"The State asked for and obtained a protective order of the questioning regarding drug use of Mr. Demmert be limited to certain time frames," Henry reminded the judge. "And that was understood clearly from day one. Unfortunately, Mr. Weidner, through a series of questions, continually violated that court order by asking Mr. Demmert questions about drug use at other times. Or asking very vague questions, which forced the State to stand up before the jury and object to Mr. Weidner's improper questions in violation of court orders."

When Weidner responded, he recited the litany that had become central to the defense argument. He mentioned Valium. He mentioned intimidation. He mentioned inaccurate statements before the grand jury. He mentioned the Fifth Amendment. He mentioned immunity.

"There has to come a time," Weidner noted, "when you have to say that you simply can't let a witness get away with this."

Judge Schulz turned away Weidner's arguments. He upheld his previous ruling on drug testimony and threatened Weidner with a contempt of court citation if he continued with that line of questioning. "If you don't like this," he told him, then appeal it to the State Court of Appeals. "The address is 333 K Street."

In a 1995 interview with this author, Schulz noted that he wasn't confident that the threat of contempt would stop Phillip Weidner. After all, not much else had. As a precaution, he asked a State Trooper to come to the courtroom. If Weidner disobeyed his orders this time, Schulz was sending him to jail.

Because it was Friday, he knew it would be until Monday before Weidner could get a judge to let him out. The trooper who showed up was Sergeant John Glass. He came in full dress uniform, ready to take Weidner away. There was no love lost between the State Troopers and Phillip Weidner. On seeing Glass, however, Weidner immediately asked to approach the bench.

"There's a State Trooper back there in his uniform," Weidner protested.

"Yeah, I know," Schulz said. "I called him."

"Well, I feel intimidated," Weidner said.

"Good," Schulz shot back. "That's exactly how I want you to feel."

21

Phillip Weidner had been perfecting his no-holds-barred style for more than a decade. Perhaps no case illustrated that better than one from 1973, when he defended a young man named Gary Zieger in the murder of a twenty-year-old woman whose semi-nude body was found stabbed in a gravel pit. The cops were already familiar with Zieger—he had been implicated in the murder of a young Alaska Native who refused to perform oral sex on him. His co-conspirator—who had bragged about the crime—was so afraid of Zieger that he refused to cooperate, even though Zieger was seen at his house just before the murder weapon mysteriously disappeared. Word on the street was that Gary Zieger was a stone-cold psychopath.

As with the current situation, the Zieger case was a circumstantial one: police had gathered more than two hundred individual items, including scene photographs, lab reports about blood found in Zieger's truck and eyewitnesses who'd seen him pick up a young woman matching the victim's appearance. In court, the defense made the most of Gary Zieger's clean-cut demeanor, and Weidner handled the circumstantial evidence with aplomb.

When a trooper took the witness stand to testify about a "blood-stained" rock found at the scene, Weidner objected. The judge directed the trooper to rephrase his answer. Sgt. Walter Gilmour delivered a mouthful, testifying that, "the rock was covered with a sticky gelatinous, red-colored, blood-like material."

A laboratory technician then testified that the blood he found in Gary Zieger's truck was human blood. Weidner asked if it was correct that his testing could prove positive for non-human blood. The answer, the technician said, was "Yes." Weidner abruptly ended his questions.

The technician got no opportunity to respond that only higher primate blood—from chimps and monkeys—would give the same reaction.

There were other mistakes and, ultimately, Phillip Weidner won an acquittal. Gary Zieger was free. Zieger went on to murder four more people—including his former boss—before being felled by a shotgun blast to the gut in a contract killing along the Seward Highway.

Having faced Phillip Weidner once before, in a vehicular homicide case that the defense specialist litigated with a landslide of motions and accusations, Henry knew she had to do something to rescue Larry Demmert's testimony from Weidner's risky, but predictable, assault. Her next witness was Sergeant Stogsdill. According to Henry, Stogsdill's testimony would be "limited solely" to his "contacts with Larry Demmert."

Stogsdill ran through the drill: he testified that Larry Demmert never appeared to be under the influence of drugs or alcohol. Insisted that police never manipulated him, that Demmert was never a suspect and denied Weidner's allegation that Demmert was told he couldn't get an attorney. Demmert had not been rehearsed for his trial testimony, Stogsdill added, and no one ever suggested answers to possible defense questions.

Weidner raised objections at every turn, a constant barrage of objections that interrupted the flow of Stogsdill's testimony and sometimes took on a personal tone. He was unyielding in his objection that Henry was introducing hearsay through Stogsdill's testimony. When it was his turn to question Stogsdill, he piled it on, attempting to drive through the restrictions that the judge had placed on the scope of Stogsdill's testimony.

"Did you participate in the initial search for evidence?" Weidner asked.

Mary Anne Henry objected and the judge sustained, reminding Weidner that the subject was Stogsdill's contact with Larry Demmert. Schulz added that questions on other subjects, "may be appropriate at a little bit later time in the trial."

Weidner was unrepentant. No sooner had the words left the judge's mouth than he asked another question designed to put the police investigation in a negative light. "But, of your testimony that you were at the scene," Weidner asked, "do you know if there was any drinking of beer by police officers in that investigation?"

"Objection, beyond the scope, and move to strike," Henry edgily responded. "And I'd ask that the jury be admonished. There is absolutely no reasonable basis in fact for the question, and it obviously is beyond the scope."

If there was one thing Phillip Weidner seemed to fear, it was loss of credibility before the jury. But when Judge Schulz sustained Henry's objection as to scope—and her motion to strike the question and admonish the jury—Weidner was at it again. "Wasn't there a substantial period of time in which you were pursuing Dean Moon as a suspect in this case?" he asked.

Mary Anne Henry objected; Schulz sustained; Weidner persisted. The judge decided the issue needed to be discussed without the jury present.

"Your Honor," Weidner protested as soon as the jury room was closed, "I've never been in a situation before where they try and call a witness for part of their testimony and then try and restrict cross-examination, but to say that they can restrict scope on whether he was actively pursuing Dean Moon and then switched to Mr. Peel is simply ludicrous.

"It goes directly to bias," the attorney added. "As to why Stogsdill gave up on Dean Moon and why he switched to Mr. Peel. And it goes directly to his bias as to whether he then tried to convince Mr. Demmert that Mr. Peel was the murderer on the 25th of March.

"Your Honor," he added, "they have put this man on for a very crucial purpose. What they want to try and do is rehabilitate Mr. Demmert."

By the time court had recessed for the day, Weidner and Henry were headed for a showdown. The issue again concerned drugs—but this time it wasn't Larry Demmert who was at the center of the controversy. This time, allegations of drug dealing by Mark Coulthurst were the cause of it all.

The trouble began when Weidner wondered aloud if perhaps Demmert's willingness to implicate John Peel had to do with his own nervousness about "furnishing drugs to a minor," the minor in question being Larry's underage girlfriend. Maybe this had caused Demmert to lie to police as to where Demmert was on the night of the murders, Weidner suggested, and that "put him in a pretty hard place" with the authorities right at a time when they were coming down on him about John Peel. Stogsdill was reluctant to agree with that characterization by the defense, but as usual, Weidner kept at him.

"Have you ever had people tell police things before in order to please them, because they may be concerned about the situation they're in?" Weidner asked. "You're aware of that, aren't you?"

"Well, I'm aware that things like that can happen," Stogsdill replied. "I don't know that I'm aware of any particular instance where it occurred to me."

Weidner immediately seized the opportunity to broaden his inquiry. "Well," he craftily suggested, "you've had informants in this case tell you that Mark Coulthurst died because…"

"Objection, your Honor," Mary Anne Henry interjected, anticipating Weidner's trajectory. "Beyond the scope."

"…he was dealing kilos of cocaine."

Henry was outraged. "Your Honor," she demanded, "I would ask that Mr. Weidner make application to the Court before he asks any questions in that nature."

In a whispered conversation at the bench, Weidner requested a hearing. He wanted to know whether he could question Alaska State Troopers about their 1984 investigation of three jail inmates who claimed to have information that linked the murders to a cocaine deal gone bad. Weidner now wanted questions about other suspects, long simmering in the background, to take their place alongside all the other controversies in this trial.

Mark Coulthurst was now as much on trial as John Peel.

22

At the following day's hearing, Weidner told the judge that three inmates had alleged Mark Coulthurst was "heavily involved in dealing cocaine" during the summer of the murders. Furthermore, the defense attorney said, the inmates claimed that Coulthurst was using the $750,000 *Investor*—which he had only recently purchased—as a fish tender from which he traded cocaine for fish. He added that Coulthurst owed $630,000 on the vessel at the time of the murders.

Henry countered Weidner's claims by telling the judge that the inmates' story—which, she said, also implicated John Peel—was baseless and "concocted by three jailhouse snitches." Indeed, Alaska authorities had used at least two of the inmates as informants in other cases. One of them was serving a sentence for possession of stolen firearms and escape. Another was serving time for rape and felony assault. The third was serving a sentence for felony theft.

But after watching the prosecution witnesses take hit after hit from Weidner, Henry wanted more. She asked Schulz to fine Weidner $500 and find him in contempt of court. He had violated a long-standing court order by asking about the inmates' story. Schulz responded that he thought he had previously ruled that attorneys could question troopers about the investigation in front of jurors.

Weidner had sharp words for Henry. "It is unfortunate," he said, "that when the prosecution feels their case slipping away they start taking pot shots at counsel." Weidner added that the story of the inmates was "not without basis." And, he said, Henry's comment that the inmates' story implicated Peel was a "red herring" designed as a "ploy for the press."

In remarks made to reporters after the day's courtroom business was finished, Henry took preemptive action. She said Weidner's suggestions were "absolutely ridiculous." The district attorney revealed that she had first become aware of the inmates' story about a month after Peel's arrest. Troopers investigated the story for two months, she added, before determining that their allegations were without merit. She went on to identify the three men in question and the origin of their allegations.

According to Henry, Barry Ewers, the man serving time for felony theft, dreamed up the story. He passed it along to James Teal, the man in jail for stolen firearms and escape, when they were in the Sitka jail. When Ewers and Teal were transferred to the Ketchikan Regional Jail, the story was relayed to Richard Hunt, who was there for rape and felony assault.

"Ewers told them the story," Henry said, "and told them maybe they could use it to make a deal" with the district attorney. Teal, whom Henry had used as an informant at a bail hearing on another murder case, and Hunt then called the district attorney at her office, setting the investigation in motion. What emerged was a fantastic tale.

As Henry told it, the inmates said Mark Coulthurst had "ripped off" someone in a drug deal. Three "hit men" from Canada were hired to kill him, the so-called "Canadian enforcers." John Peel was the "go-between," she said, who showed the hit men around Craig. According to the informants, Peel took the hit men to the *Investor* on the night of the murders. Peel also kidnapped Mark Coulthurst's 4-year-old son, John, at the time the rest of the crew was murdered, and killed him later. The inmates also claimed it was Peel who burned the *Investor* two days after the murders.

Henry told reporters that troopers talked to Teal and Hunt, then tracked down Barry Ewers in Seattle. From there, they went to Canada and talked to the three men Teal had identified as the hit men. They all had alibis, Henry said, adding, "They were flabbergasted. One of them had loaned Ewers $100 and never got it back."

At that point, Henry said, "it was obvious that Ewers was feeding them information, that he had made up the story, and that Teal and Hunt were embellishing it from news reports." She decided to drop Teal as an informant in the other murder case, moreover, when she learned that Ewers had also fed him information on that case. Henry added, it was now important that the story fabricated by the inmates be explained to the jurors, since the subject was brought up during the questioning of Stogsdill.

"The jurors now think that Mark Coulthurst maybe was involved with cocaine and I was trying to hide it because I objected and the witness didn't get to answer," Henry said. "It's one of Phil's tactics."

"They know they can't prove this," she continued. "I'd love to see them call the two snitches to the stand."

Weidner responded to Henry's remarks by stubbornly sticking to his original allegations. Under the circumstances, he said, he intended to "pursue the failure of officers to adequately investigate reports by the state's own informants that Mark Coulthurst died due to his involvement in cocaine trafficking."

The man simply refused to flinch. Still, his tactics could only be described as brazen. Each time the inmates talked, the more absurd their stories became. No one revealed that better than Richard Hunt.

Rick Hunt's first letter to Judge Schulz arrived in late January 1986, while the judge was in the midst of jury selection. He wrote in a jailhouse scrawl that tumbled across a page filled with misspelled words. He begged Judge Schulz to believe him.

Your Honor.

My name is Richard J. Hunt and I'm writeing to you about the Peel case. Since the first day of these merders I've made statements against Berry Yours [Barry Ewers], Berry's wife and family and John Peel. I saw John Peel, Berry's wife's brother and uncel merder and berry that little boy in Petersburg. I no were he is berryed write now do you care?

The merder weapon belonged to Berry Yours. He was working for the D.A. These people are devil worshipers and big time cocaine smugglers but all the powers of darkness won't help them and all there money won't save them. God is useing me agines them. Sir, please please beleave me.

The Investor was selling cocaine. The cops sent people like Berry aboard with marked money. Why won't no one listen to me.

Schulz received another missive from the inmate on February 3, 1986. This time, Hunt was determined not to leave out anything. After insisting that he was an innocent man—and that "every word I've said is fact and truth," Hunt had launched into a finely crafted tale that matched Mary Anne Henry's subsequent court and newspaper accounts to the word. He repeated his tale of drug deals gone bad, of an organized crime group called "The Family," and implicated John Peel in the robbery and arson of the *Investor*.

In July of 1984, Hunt's tale continued, he ran into Barry Ewers in Petersburg—and Ewers was none too happy. According to Hunt, Ewers accused him of "shooting my mouth off'" about the *Investor* murders. Hunt denied the accusations, but Ewers "said his family knew better and that if I didn't leave town fast and the country, I was dead." Based on that threat, Hunt said, he and his brother decided to leave for Oregon.

As soon as Hunt left Petersburg, though, he ran into problems. Spinning his story to new heights, Hunt alleged that the Barry Ewers crime family subsequently made false accusations against him. Everything that had gone wrong in his life, it seemed, could be blamed on Barry Ewers. "Within 24 hours of leaving Petersburg," Hunt said, "I was arrested for raping a girl."

Like many a man before and after him, Rick Hunt was willing to trade his "inside knowledge" for a ticket to freedom or, at the very least, a more lenient sentence. Judge Schulz, for one, had not taken the bait.

When Schulz responded to Hunt's second letter, he was extremely blunt. Hunt got only two lines: "I have received your letter mailed February 3," the judge wrote. "As you requested, I have supplied a copy to the parties involved in the Peel case."

If Schulz had thought that was the end of it, he had been sadly mistaken. Rick Hunt and his jailhouse buddies would live on as rumors, innuendoes and harbingers of reasonable doubt. They were more important outside the courtroom than in it.

23

Ketchikan, Alaska
April 1986

Sue Domenowske had seen the skiffman on the cold storage dock. She'd spoken to him. Now married to Paul Page and going by her married name of Domenowske-Page, she didn't much want to be in the courtroom. She'd gone eye-to-eye with the man presumed to have been the killer. He had been free for at least two years and each year she had grown more afraid.

Her darkest realization came in December 1983, when Stogsdill visited her remote cabin in Hollis, on the opposite side of Prince of Wales Island from Craig. Stogsdill had arrived by chartered floatplane with additional photos for her and Paul Page to review, with new line-ups that finally included John Peel. Stogsdill knew they weren't starting with a clean slate. Those two had already seen dozens of photos. It was the best he could do.

While the floatplane waited, Stogsdill started Sue off with the line-ups. Her house, still under construction, was without a full-time heater and it was cold. That late in December the temperature hovered in the teens. When Page showed up, Stogsdill told him he could stay while Sue looked at the photos.

"Does that mean I can build a fire?" Sue laughed. Then she turned serious, revealing the fear that had hounded her since her chance conversation with a killer.

"How did my name get released and in all the papers?" she'd asked. She had reason to be concerned. Whoever had done this deed was still at large. She was a witness. Anyone who could read knew who she was and, presumably, where to find her. Stogsdill did his best to explain. It didn't help.

By the time he left, though, she'd pointed to a surveillance photo of John Peel and noted that it looked very similar to the skiffman. "What bothers me," she said at the time, "is the hair seems too light. But I'd say this individual is very similar looking to the fellow we saw," adding almost absent-mindedly, "But I can't say positively it's him."

Being in the courtroom now, face to face with the suspect, did nothing to assuage her fear. Taking the stand, she told the jury that the skiffman "looked like a dirty fisherman coming in who needed to take a shower." She estimated that she had a three-minute conversation with him. Asked to describe the man, the janitor and special education teacher said he was slim and muscular, with thin, stringy brown hair, an "ugly" chin that was set back and a handful of "bad pimples" on his face. He appeared to be in shock, she added.

Of all the witnesses, Domenowske-Page had the most detailed memory. Assistant prosecutor Pat Gullufsen took his time with the young woman, sticking to general questions about what she'd seen. Eventually he came to the crucial question. He asked her if John Peel resembled the skiff operator.

Sue Domenowske-Page spent 45 seconds staring silently at the Bellingham fisherman, who stood up at Gullufsen's request. She asked—and was permitted—to view Peel from a side angle. Asked if John Peel resembled the skiff operator, she said, "In some respects, yes."

She thought his hair was too light, but thought the shape of his eyebrows and eyes was similar. She was uncomfortable with his eye color, but testified that his mouth mannerisms when he took a drink of water reminded her of the skiff operator. As she began to describe similarities between Peel's mouth and the mouth of the skiff operator, however, she became upset. Judge Schulz called a recess and Domenowske-Page was led, grimacing and near tears, out of the courtroom.

When she returned, Judge Schulz noticed that the jury was distracted. But not by the witness. They were distracted by Phillip Weidner: he was slowly, methodically, stroking his beard. Schulz noticed that no one in the room was listening to Domenowske-Page, except the prosecution attorneys. Domenowske-Page, meanwhile, returned to the subject of John Peel. She said Peel appeared to have a belly, while the skiffman did not, then added that, "I see a lot of similarity."

Almost by impulse, Gullufsen showed her a color photograph of John Peel. He was fairly certain the witness had never seen it before. The picture, taken by one of Peel's friends during a past fishing season, showed him holding the tiller of a boat and staring into the camera.

"I'd say that's a picture of the skiff operator," Domenowske-Page said to the surprise of everyone in the courtroom. "That's the skiff operator." She moved back noticeably in her chair as she made the revelation.

Peel's attorneys immediately requested that the photo not be shown to the jurors, claiming that to show the witness only one photo was suggestive. "They got more identification on the picture than they did in court," Brant McGee argued, unsuccessfully. "They're trying to bolster their lack of an in-court ID."

When McGee got his turn at Domenowske-Page, he picked at her seeming willingness to change her ranking of a potential suspect during a December 1982 interview with Sergeant Chuck Miller in Seattle. The woman admitted that she "had a gut feeling against" Miller, whom she had taken a dislike to during a 1976 encounter in Fairbanks. But she denied that Miller's "pushy'" attitude and her desire to "just get him to leave" her mother's home had led her to increase her rating of a suspect from a "five" to a "seven."

Miller didn't "talk me from a five to a seven," Domenowske-Page countered. "The picture really struck home at a gut level."

By the time Sue Domenowske-Page left the stand, a week had passed. At the end of that weeklong parade, the prosecution asked all six of its eyewitnesses to identify the mysterious skiffman in one way or another. Most of them—including Joe Weiss, the *only* witness who started off with the full complement of lineup photos—were cautious in their testimony, saying things like, "Peel looks a lot like the guy," or "I'm pretty sure he could be the skiffman."

Judge Schulz wondered why they had bothered. Of the six, only Sue Domenowske-Page identified John Peel with any certainty.

24

Ketchikan, Alaska
April 1986

Trooper Bob Anderson thought the Peel trial had lost its way. He thought he knew why: neither the court nor the state knew how to handle Weidner's street-fighting defense tactics. From Anderson's point of view, Judge Schulz lacked the experience—and expertise— to keep Peel's scrappy attorney under control. He thought the prosecution, on the other hand, was afraid they'd do something wrong and John Peel would get off on appeal. Everyone in the system, it seemed, was being overly cautious.

Trooper Anderson's frustration finally got to the point that he blew up at Mary Anne Henry. "We're responding too much to Weidner's theories and accusations," he told her. "Every time he comes up with a new one, we send an investigator on a wild goose chase to check it out. Every time we do that," he said, "we make it look like we're not confident in our case.

"What we need to do," he continued, "is get back and present our case. We shouldn't let all these theories, and things Weidner is doing, muddy the waters and cause us to overreact."

But Mary Anne Henry knew something else. She'd been in Craig during the early days of the investigation. Was at Trooper Anderson's house when things blew up over the way the investigation was being handled. Had seen and heard the intimations that the on-shore trooper investigation in Craig was less than stellar. Had witnessed the heated dispute over who should be in charge. It was water over the gunnels at this point, but the effects had been far-reaching.

135

On the witness stand, Anderson at least had a chance to take the focus off the legal folderol. He would tell the jurors that the first fire call came at 4:20 or 4:25 in the afternoon. He would tell them of the impossibilities he faced as he raced around Craig looking for fire equipment. He would take them to the *Investor* scene. He knew the sights. He knew the smells. The jurors would finally see the heinous crime and understand its enormity. Trooper Anderson had touched the victims.

Phillip Weidner never missed a beat; when it came his turn to cross-examine the trooper, he was ready to pounce. Trooper Anderson presented him with his first unambiguous chance to attack the police investigation and the defense attorney left no doubt as to where the attack would begin.

Weidner started by having the trooper write out a list of things he could have fingerprinted—but didn't. The next thing Weidner got Anderson to admit was that troopers might have "stacked the deck" against John Peel by putting eight of his pictures in a photographic line-up that contained less than thirty photos. Even with these admissions, Weidner was far from finished.

He insinuated that Anderson had destroyed a page in his trooper notebook. He based his opinion on the observation that the trooper made no entries in his notebook from 2:30 on the afternoon of the fire to 7:30 that night. And yet, Weidner pointed out, he had made detailed entries up to that point. Anderson explained, sensibly, that he wasn't writing in his notebook because he was busy doing other things.

If Trooper Anderson had to answer for the initial fire call, Chuck Miller got stuck with the dubious duty of relating the messy first year of the investigation. Since his involvement had started at Ben's Cove where the *Investor* had burned—not in town—his initial testimony promised to evolve into a detailed catalog of the evidence they'd found on the boat. Routine stuff that could quickly get mired in detail. In Judge Schulz's courtroom, though, hardly anything was routine.

In Miller's case, it took only a half hour or so before things heated up. The cause was crime scene and crew photographs Mary Anne Henry wanted to introduce into evidence, photographs she wanted Miller to describe. Weidner objected. Vigorously.

The photographs, he said, were "of burned remains and I think they're unduly prejudicial." The offending photographs showed a protruding bone, which Weidner found "pretty gruesome." Citing a general rule of inadmissibility on "so-called gruesome photographs," Weidner argued they shouldn't come in as evidence. "I think it's clearly an effort to inflame the jury to instill undue prejudice in them," he told the judge.

Mary Anne Henry won the skirmish by arguing that the photo of the corpse wasn't "recognizable as a human being," hence "not gruesome" and not "prejudicial." Had she wanted to inflame the jury, she added, she would have had "Trooper Anderson go into gruesome detail about the bodies he found, because those bodies were at least recognizable as human beings."

For the rest of the day, and most of the next, Miller offered evidence and explanations. The evidence came first and there was plenty. On the first day alone, Miller went through nearly one hundred evidence photos taken on the *Investor*. If there was a flaw to Miller's performance, it was that sometimes jurors had a hard time seeing the photos. And then, when testimony turned to firearms, Phillip Weidner let him have it.

"He's not an expert," the defense attorney complained. "The man's not an expert." The judge let the cop talk but, with three nearly identical objections in three minutes, Weidner got his point across.

And then they showed a videotape from Channel 13 in Anchorage, showing Miller, Stogsdill and Anderson screening and sifting debris at Ben's Cove, in the rain. The jury saw the twisted shape of the blackened boat and the long shrimp screens that took shovelfuls from the gritty burned out hulk. What the jury saw was, for Miller, the most remarkable thing of all. The *Investor* killer hadn't exactly intended to make his job easy. The fire was meant to destroy everything. The killer had nearly succeeded.

Every minute the boat burned, evidence was destroyed. Yet somehow, within that mess, Miller had found bones—human bones— and he'd found teeth. Teeth that a forensic dentist had used to identify the unidentifiable. Chris Heyman. Dean Moon.

"The scene investigation paid off," he said privately, "if only because we were able to find Dean Moon's tooth."

Expecting to be asked the "fingerprint" question, Miller had an explanation for that, too. Miller said all the fingerprint techniques available to him "could not be applied simply because of what had happened on the *Investor*." The heat of the fire, he believed, would have evaporated the body oils making up the fingerprint impression. Prints on the skiff, meanwhile, would likely be partial prints, in part because most surfaces on the skiff "represented very limited surfaces."

"On the other hand," he continued from the witness stand, "I knew that I had four eyewitnesses, and at that point I suppose you have to make a decision. The decision I made at that point was this: the issue was going to be confused regardless, later on down the line, but in my judgment at that time, because of the fact that it was unattended, and because I may have detected prints that would never have been identified, I chose not to do it and rely on the eyewitnesses instead."

In another jab at the defense, Miller scoffed at the notion the killings had been performed by a professional hit man. The purpose of a contract killing, he said, was to let the deaths be known. A professional wouldn't stick around for two days trying to destroy his message, Miller told jurors. He also discounted the involvement of a stranger in the murders, because in his experience most murders were committed by a family member or someone who knew the victim. The burning of the *Investor*, he added, "implies an association between the killer and the crime scene." Strangers don't destroy crime scenes, he concluded.

And then there was the question of Dean Moon. Miller said that by the time Stogsdill took over the case in 1983, Moon "was fading in my mind" as a suspect. "I felt he would have surfaced by that time, he would have contacted his family," if he had survived, Miller added.

Undeterred, and unfazed, Weidner worked at unraveling Miller's testimony. He started by questioning the trooper's objectivity. He dug at the cop's decision not to fingerprint the *Investor* and wondered if the troopers hadn't managed to lose crucial evidence. In a wide-ranging, free form romp through his notes, Weidner also suggested that the murders might have occurred when the *Investor* was anchored in Ben's Cove. After all, Weidner suggested, hadn't a Craig resident heard gunshots, "every hour on the hour" while the *Investor* was out at Fish Egg Island?

"Do you have any physical evidence that would prove in any

manner that they weren't being simply held prisoner and they were taken out to the cove for some reason?" Weidner slyly asked. "Perhaps to force Mr. Coulthurst to do something?"

Miller had his doubts. The tie lines left behind by the *Investor* told him something had gone wrong before they hit Ben's Cove. The fact that the family didn't leave town on Monday, as they were supposed to, told him the same thing. The woman who heard the gunshots, meanwhile, lived more than a mile from the scene. The sound of a .22 rifle wouldn't have carried that far, even across the water.

Yet Miller had to admit there was no physical evidence to prove that the murders had occurred the previous night in Craig. There was no physical evidence to prove much of anything, except that people had died. "That went when the boat burned," he reminded the jury. That was the problem. That had always been the problem.

Sgt. Stogsdill's second trip to the stand at the end of April promised to be a lengthy one. Each side had their agenda—the state to present him as the glue that bound the pieces of their circumstantial case, the defense to show him as a reckless man who had rushed to judgment. His six days in Judge Schulz's courtroom provided the opportunity for all this and more.

In his first three days of testimony, Stogsdill played the role of chronicler, taking over where Sergeant Miller left off. He spoke of the fire and his arson investigation. He talked at length about how the investigation wandered in the wilderness for its first year, because "we didn't have identifiable remains for two of the crewmen." He also spoke of John Peel, and how troopers came to focus on him as their chief suspect.

The defense, meanwhile, spent an entire day on a foray into the murky waters of drugs and drug dealing. Weidner again charged that troopers didn't thoroughly investigate reports that Mark Coulthurst and Dean Moon were involved in drug trafficking. He asked Stogsdill to answer allegations that Moon had "ripped someone off for $20,000 to $30,000 in cocaine money," had stolen marijuana plants from a grow and could put together deals for "any kind of drugs."

"We checked that story out," Stogsdill replied. The guy who made the allegation was six years older than Moon, even though he claimed to be a high school buddy. No local authorities, including the

Mounties, discovered any link between Dean Moon and drugs. The man's allegations, Stogsdill said, "appeared to be an isolated incident."

By mid-morning, Mary Anne Henry had heard enough. She requested Weidner be fined for violating court rules with questions about drugs and Dean Moon. Henry added that the defense should offer evidence of drug allegations against Mark Coulthurst, or be prevented from putting such questions to witnesses. Schulz took Peel and Weidner into chambers and reprimanded the attorneys. But he declined to fine Phillip Weidner. Schulz' loss of control over his own courtroom was now near total.

25

Inside the courtroom and out, John Peel was a sphinx, a cipher, a near specter who had little to say for himself. The impression was that Weidner exercised considerable control over his client. Both the judge and the prosecution had seen the attorney continually intervene on Peel's behalf, even trying to prevent Peel from answering "yes" or "no" questions.

The practice was particularly noticeable when Peel was waiving his rights, as he did when he waived his right to testify at trial. Judge Schulz had to pressure Peel to get him to personally enter the waiver, as the rules required. Phillip Weidner even wanted to put his own name on the record when Peel put forward his final waiver of the right to testify.

The closest the jury ever came to hearing Peel speak for himself was in January 1986, when Peel—at the behest of his attorneys—asked to add himself as co-counsel. The task of presenting that request fell to Brant McGee. As McGee explained, admitting Peel as co-counsel would allow the defendant to question witnesses and address the judge. What McGee didn't point out was that, as co-counsel, John Peel could make statements in court without having to worry about being cross-examined by the prosecution. Schulz never gave him the chance.

Indeed, John Peel's best voice in the courtroom was his wife's dogged appearance through the long course of the trial, sometimes with their child in tow. Much had been made of John Peel's questionable character, including his drug dealing, a Craig dalliance with another woman and a Ketchikan encounter with a prostitute. In a strange way, her husband's "bad character" worked to his advantage, because it provided an alternate explanation as to why he went missing during the two days surrounding the murders. The defense made sure Cathy

Peel was in court whenever her husband's character was questioned. She sat by stoically, never reacting one way or the other to the evidence.

John Peel's family was also speaking for him in the court of public opinion. Cathy Peel said her husband's personality did not change after the murders, although he became increasingly upset over persistent questioning by Alaska State Troopers, who considered him a prime suspect in the case. "He slept well," Cathy said. "There was no change at all. He was the same John Peel."

Marilyn Peel told the *Bellingham Herald* about a family trip in the days after the murders. She said that her son was his normal self on the drive to Reno, during which the deaths were discussed. "He was relaxed," Marilyn Peel said. "If he was supposed to have committed eight murders..."

She added that, "we were all sick about it. I remember him saying that he could understand [an *Investor* crewmember] getting mad enough to [harm] him [Mark Coulthurst]. But Irene and the kids?"

John Peel's silence did not last forever. It all changed when his March 24, 1984, interview with Sergeants Flothe and Galyan was cleared for jury presentation. On appeal, Schulz' ruling to suppress the interview was overturned by the State Court of Appeals. By mid-April 1986, Schulz issued another ruling: he would admit all but a fourteen-minute portion of the tape into evidence.

The portion that was omitted focused on John Peel talking to himself just after agreeing to take the polygraph exam. The rest of the excluded portion included the results of that examination, which indicated that John Peel had been "deceptive" when he denied killing Mark Coulthurst. Interestingly enough, the defense also claimed to have a polygraph of John Peel; that they even mentioned it was proof he had passed that exam. Judge Schulz declined to admit that tape as well.

Against that background, Sergeant Flothe barely spoke of the missing fourteen minutes when he testified about Peel's Bellingham interview. The closest he came was in response to a carefully phrased series of questions from Mary Anne Henry. She asked him if, during the interview, John Peel was left alone so he could "calm down."

"Yes," Flothe answered.

"Was that a substantial period of time?" she asked.

"Yes," Flothe replied.

Still, the sergeant was not rendered mute on the stand. He explained, in perhaps the most succinct way yet, how the investigation had come to focus on John Peel. He was being asked about the "anniversary meetings" in Ketchikan and Craig. What was the "purpose" of those meetings, Mary Anne Henry wondered.

"I think the purpose and the thrust, at that time," Flothe recalled, "was that the investigation for quite some time had been focused on the fact that maybe the suspect was from aboard the *Investor*. Dean Moon or Chris Heyman. And there hadn't been a lot of work done as far as looking away from crewmen and determining if someone else, not on board the boat, might be responsible. And we felt that we should check that out."

The set piece in this drama, though, was the Flothe and Galyan interview in Bellingham. The plan, Flothe said, was to confront John Peel with his responsibility for the crimes. By doing so, the trooper noted, they hoped either to "obtain some admissions, or confession, or perhaps he would give us an alibi that we could clear him with."

They got neither.

But now, through the magic of technology, the jury would finally hear John Peel speak for himself.

26

Ketchikan, Alaska
May 1986

Dawn Holmstrom had heard John Peel make what seemed to be incriminating statements in the days after the murders. She had testified before the grand jury that he was missing from their boat in the days surrounding the murders. But Mary Anne Henry wanted Dawn Holmstrom declared an "adverse witness." She was biased toward John Peel, Henry claimed. They had been boyfriend-girlfriend, she noted, "though for some reason she's denying it now."

Worse yet, Holmstrom had recanted a crucial portion of her grand jury testimony, Henry said, "after speaking to the defendant's brother, Robert Peel." There was more to it than that, though. Dawn Holmstrom and Brian Polinkus had gone to a private attorney after their first grand jury appearance, alleging mistreatment at the hands of Bob Blasco and Detective Dave McNeill—mistreatment that Holmstrom said had led her to testify erroneously.[14]

There was no question that officials had been forceful as they prepped her for the grand jury. Holmstrom had already tantalized them with her report of an emotional conversation with Peel at Ruth

14   When Dawn Holmstrom returned to Bellingham after the first Grand Jury she was upset, and told her father about her interview with the authorities. Her father told her she should get an attorney and took her to see Phillip Rosellini, a former chief criminal deputy in the Spokane County, Washington, prosecuting attorney's office. When Brian Polinkus learned of Dawn's meeting with Rosellini, he too decided he wanted to talk to the attorney. The result of their meetings with the Bellingham attorney was an October 18 letter alleging prosecutorial intimidation. Judge Schulz investigated the claims, but never found them credible.

Ann's on the morning after the fire. As they headed into the grand jury, they wanted details. Unfortunately, Holmstrom had evidenced difficulty in remembering what was said. So much trouble that, at one point, Detective McNeill suggested she might have a "mind block." Holmstrom kept insisting that she couldn't remember what was said. McNeill had been equally adamant that she try to remember.

"I can't," she told him. "I can't."

"I can't," McNeill repeated, mocking her. "I can't."

Dawn Holmstrom finally let out snippets of her post-fire conversation with John Peel during her grand jury appearance; it was a halting, stuttering affair, the words barely escaping her lips. Her biggest trouble seemed to be remembering the conversation in which John Peel was supposed to have "confessed." Bob Blasco had again tried to coax it out of her.

"Dawn," Blasco said after a series of preliminary questions, "put yourself at Ruth Ann's and tell the grand jury what he said."

"He started crying," she had said, looking toward the grand jurors for the first time. "And I went—and he told me that it all happened so fast. That he couldn't believe that he did it."

"What else did he say, Dawn?" Blasco asked.

Dawn had been taken elsewhere by the reality of her revelation. She had just given her friend up to the grand jury. She seemed lost. Bob Blasco tried to bring her back; he implored her to respond by saying, "Dawn?" Holmstrom ignored him. Finally, the assistant district attorney said, "Take your time." That seemed to bring her around.

" 'I can't believe I could have done that,' " she said, this time seeming to quote John Peel. Then she added, "He said that it happened so fast that he couldn't believe he did it."

"Were you scared, Dawn?" Blasco had wondered.

"Yes."

"What about him scared you?"

"His eyes," she replied. She was talking about the news photos of John Peel in Bellingham, his eyes piercing out from behind a ski mask.

Those incriminating statements were now, at trial, something she wanted to take back. Over defense objections, Judge Schulz declared Dawn Holmstrom an adverse witness. She testified under immunity from perjury charges for five lines of changed testimony. That maneuver didn't solve the problem of Dawn Holmstrom any more than declaring her an adverse witness did.

On the witness stand, Dawn Holmstrom was a cute 23-year-old with a turned up nose and spaced-out demeanor. After all the rough fishermen faces, she was a contrast of femininity. But Dawn Holmstrom had the perfect excuse. Even armed with every one of Holmstrom's many contradictory statements, Henry was ill prepared to counteract the woman's simple evasion. When things got tough, Dawn Holmstrom simply said, "I can't remember."

Mary Anne Henry asked her if she remembered telling troopers that, "John was depressed towards the end of the summer."

"I could have," Holmstrom answered. "I don't know. That's possible. That's been a long time."

Mary Anne Henry asked her if she remembered, "telling Detective McNeill that John Peel had gone downhill since the murders."

"Not exactly, no," Holmstrom replied.

"Well, what did you say?" Henry asked.

"I don't know," the young woman replied.

When Henry asked about the crucial morning rendezvous with Peel at Ruth Ann's, Holmstrom's memory turned increasingly vague. Exasperated, Henry said, "You were at Ruth Ann's for thirty to 45 minutes and you can't tell us anything that you said to John Peel or he said to you?"

"I can't remember," Holmstrom declared.

For two days, the jury was out of the courtroom as much as in. Each time the delay was brought on by Henry's questions of Holmstrom and Brant McGee's objections. During one of those confrontations, Holmstrom leaned her head against the side of the witness stand and closed her eyes. By the end of the second day, Mary Anne Henry and Brant McGee had both been fined $50.00 for fighting at Schulz's bench. Both paid with personal checks.

By day three, Dawn Holmstrom had been on the witness stand three days too many. Henry led her through a tedious rendition of every contradictory statement she had ever uttered about the *Investor* fire. The only purpose for the exercise seemed to be a set up for another prosecution zinger. Henry sneered, "Has anybody ever told you that you have to have a good memory when you make up a story, so that your facts in that story are always straight?"

"I don't think that's a story," Holmstrom shot back.

When Brant McGee started cross-examination in the middle of the third day, his task was greatly simplified by Holmstrom's extensive time on the stand. She appeared worn out, her eyes and face downcast, her voice softer than it had been with Mary Anne Henry. Asked if she had been pushed around by police officers in her pre-grand jury interview, she replied, "I'm easily pushed around by anyone."

She insisted she had no reason to give Peel an alibi, because she didn't know he was a suspect when she first told authorities of the bank incident. She said she started to think Peel was a suspect after a February 1984 interview, during which police asked pointed questions about her friend.

"Did you figure it out for yourself?" McGee asked.

"I'm a lot smarter than people think I am," Holmstrom insisted.

Judge Schulz wondered whether the state needed Dawn Holmstrom's testimony as badly as they seemed to think. They knew what kind of witness she was going to be at trial, because they'd taken her deposition—a debacle they'd only been able to escape with his assistance. To Schulz's thinking, the world would have been a lot better for Dawn Holmstrom had she never gotten involved in the trial. Perhaps, he concluded, Dawn Holmstrom just wanted out. She knew too many people who were involved.

27

Ketchikan, Alaska

Trouble was brewing among jury members. The problem first surfaced in mid-May, when one of the jurors was dismissed because he didn't want to miss the start of the salmon fishing season. The issue surfaced again on June 9th, when Schulz dismissed juror Julane Kirkpatrick, who became the third juror to leave the panel.

By June 10, 1986, one of the jurors started circulating a letter that asked for more jury pay and hinted that the jury was "distracted by worries about domestic and financial commitments."

On June 18th, Schulz received the letter that had been circulating among the jury for a week. The typed missive was signed by eight of the fifteen remaining jurors and alternates. The news was not good.

"Dear Sir," the letter started, as it outlined the jurors' concerns.

> Due to the length of this trial, State of Alaska vs. John Peel, many of the jury are experiencing financial and domestic hardships.
>
> The trial itself is now in the fourth month of a predicted 3-4 months. At this point, the State has not even finished calling its witnesses. With the remainder of the State's witnesses, all of the defense witnesses, plus the deliberations, we feel that we are looking at a minimum of six weeks, but more probably over two months before a verdict can be reached.
>
> Those of us who were looking for work at the time of the *voir dire* were hoping that [our] request for $100.00/day

jury pay would be approved. Since Ketchikan has a largely seasonal employment economy, we are going to be losing most of our expected annual income.

We all realize the importance of the American Trial Process and feel a deep commitment to do our part... If the State of Alaska would take the unforeseeable difficulties of this jury's situation into consideration and raised our compensation to about $75.00/day, it would certainly help to ease our mental distress while doing our civic duty.

The jury had spoken and the dissenters were plainly in the majority. Schulz was listening. Acting quickly, he asked each juror to write down precisely how the trial's length had affected him or her. He would use their responses to formulate an appropriate response. After reading the jury's letters, many of which complained about lost wages and increased expenses, Judge Schulz decided to request higher payment for the jury.

On July 11, 1986—eleven days after Schulz's request—the jurors received the decision of Art Snowden, Administrative Director of the Superior Court system. In his response, Snowden noted that Administrative Rule 14 allowed the administrative director to "authorize different pay schedules when circumstances dictate." He added, however, that this provision "has never been invoked to authorize additional payment to jurors in a lengthy trial due to resulting financial hardship."

"This office recognizes that the jurors in this unusual case have devoted hundreds of hours to the performance of their civic duty," Snowden noted. "Certainly these jurors deserve the heartfelt thanks of the people of Alaska for their willingness to serve on a jury for this length of time."

"However," he continued, "an examination of the jurors' statements reveals that several jurors are not suffering any financial hardship as a result of the current pay schedule. Other jurors have speculated that they may have found employment had they not been engaged in the trial, but they have not presented any showing or assurance that they would have been employed."

"Based upon the information presented to this office at this time," the administrative director determined, "I cannot conclude that the extraordinary action of approving a blanket payment increase in juror fees is justified." Snowden did make one concession to the jurors who were experiencing hardship, however.

"Jurors who are incurring definite, verifiable out-of-pocket losses may present claims to this office after the conclusion of the trial," Snowden said. But he didn't make any guarantees. No one, it seemed, could make guarantees. Some of the jurors might receive extra pay. Some might not. The trial would end when it ended.

28

Ketchikan, Alaska
Wednesday, June 18 - Friday, June 20, 1986

After months of being at the periphery of the case, the Coulthurst family was finally summoned to Ketchikan. They could not enter the courtroom, however, until after they'd testified. John and Sally Coulthurst brought their eldest daughter Laurie[15], to lend moral support. Daughter Lisa, who'd just had her tonsils out, joined them the next day. She made it just in time: Ketchikan and its airport were soon socked in with fog.

John and Sally Coulthurst arrived in court convinced that John Peel was the killer. As the trial progressed, they had grown to believe their son was on trial, not Peel. Their confidence was hardly boosted when prosecutors told them not to show emotion in the courtroom. But nothing could have prepared them for their ordeal.

Indeed, of the four Coulthursts, Lisa was probably the luckiest. Still recovering from surgery, she gobbled Tylenol 3's for her throat. She didn't go to the courtroom. She didn't do anything except look at the fog. But she wasn't that lucky. Mark's death had sent Lisa into a tailspin. The shock of it was so great that she went straight immediately, forswearing drugs and alcohol. When John Peel was arrested, Lisa Coulthurst fell apart. Then she met the man who saved her cookies. After they married in 1983, Lisa left the U.S., moved to Canada and got out of the loop. The change did her good. She was able to muddle through the day without the distractions of cops and reporters and other total strangers.

---

15   Not to be confused with Laurie *Hudson*, who was Irene Hudson Coulthurst's sister.

Laurie Coulthurst who, like her sister, was not scheduled to testify, took a vantage point that afforded her a good view of the defendant. She was shocked by what she saw. John Peel hardly looked like John Peel. This wasn't the grubby person she'd seen fishing with her brother or drunk at parties. This was Joe College. Even as a kid he hadn't looked like that.

With everyone else in her family sidelined, Laurie had become the *de facto* family spokeswoman. She told reporters she had heard John was the prime suspect months earlier. But didn't want to believe it. "Johnny Peel" was one of the guys, she said; someone she regarded as friendly and outgoing, with a sense of humor. "I really want to give John the benefit of the doubt," she reported. "But I really want someone to be arrested and put away. I'm really torn."

Laurie publicly counted the toll her brother's murder had taken. She had been in counseling for two years, she told the reporter, and still the murders haunted her. She suffered from headaches and a nervous stomach, she added. She had recently woken up crying after dreaming that her brother was back. "This is coming up all over again," she said. "I want it all finished."

She had only one fear: that she would be unable to look at John Peel when she got to the courtroom. "I wish it would have been some crazy off the boat," she confessed. "I've been wanting to hate someone for the past two years."

Laurie then confessed to the reporter that she'd told her mother, "If it's someone we know, I hope he's not sentenced to death." Then she said, "I wouldn't want death for the person. There have been too many deaths."

Of the two parents, John Coulthurst had the dubious honor of testifying first. Most of Bob Blasco's questions were foundational. "How did Mark get into commercial fishing?" Blasco asked. "What were the names of his boats?" John Coulthurst was his usual self: blunt yet gracious. He maintained that attitude when the subject turned to John Peel.

"That's true," he answered when Blasco asked him if Peel was a friend of his daughter Lisa. And yes, John Coulthurst added, his son had fired John Peel.[16]

---

16   The Peel family steadfastly denied that John had been fired. They countered that John decided to quit fishing with Mark Coulthurst because *The Kit* was not seaworthy. Indeed, John Peel helped save *The Kit* from sinking during his last season with Mark.

"And how do you know that?" Blasco asked.

"My son told me so," the senior Coulthurst replied.

John Coulthurst also testified he'd seen Peel two or three times at the Cocoanut Grove tavern in Bellingham. All Peel had said was, "Hi." Not once did he ask how the investigation was going, though other people did. When they got to what was to be the climactic John Peel question, however, Bob Blasco stumbled.

He wanted to ask John Coulthurst whether John Peel had ever told him he wasn't responsible for killing his son. In a conversation, it's an easy question to ask. In a courtroom, such questions require foundation, which is lawyer-speak for background and contextual information. Blasco tried to skip the background the first time around. Weidner took it to the bench and Judge Schulz made Blasco start over. Blasco hardly did better the second time around. He added a month, day and year to the equation, but the question was the same: "Did John Peel ever come to you, John Coulthurst, and say, 'I didn't kill your son, I didn't kill your daughter-in-law, I didn't kill your grandchildren...' "

Weidner again objected. The judge instructed the jury about the prosecution's "improper conduct." Blasco took offense and asked to approach the bench. An increasingly impatient Schulz turned him back. By the time the question was acceptably framed, Blasco asked only whether John Peel had ever come to the Coulthurst house or talked to him about the murders.

"No, he did not," John Coulthurst, answered.

When Phillip Weidner took over, John Coulthurst said, "I do not know," "He did not" and "Never" more frequently. The defense attorney posed questions that asked if his son lied on his loan application for the *Investor*. Or questions designed to get the elder Coulthurst to say nice things about John Peel. For the defense, the answers seemed to matter less than the questions.

While John Coulthurst was confident as he entered the courtroom, Sally Coulthurst teetered. She was so nervous her microphone fell apart on her blouse, its clip broken. But Sally Coulthurst had plenty to say, mostly about her son and his estate, but also about John Peel. Bob Blasco had her tell the story of an encounter she'd had with John Peel in the year after the murders.

Sally Coulthurst responded that she had confronted Peel with information he had "sold dope to Dean Moon and Jerome Keown" on the night of the murders. She urged him to tell the troopers about the incident, assuring him that "they won't do anything to you." But John Peel hadn't answered her, Sally Coulthurst told the jury. He had walked away.

"I walked over and talked to him again," Sally told the jury. "And I said, 'You know, Dean Moon was seen alive in San Francisco,' and his eyes just bugged out and he just looked at me and that was it."

Sally Coulthurst's testimony on Mark Coulthurst's estate, meanwhile, had only one purpose: to show Mark Coulthurst as a hard-working, successful fisherman. She said her son's estate was worth $566,664.83 at his death. After paying off his debts and liabilities, the estate was worth $334,968.35. Of that, $100,000 was in unpaid fish tickets from the bankrupt Holbeck Fish Company.

When Weidner took over, he elected to remain seated, rather than stand while pawing through stacks of legal folders. He was aware, no doubt, that it wouldn't sit well with the jury if he appeared to be badgering the victim's mother. Sally Coulthurst still ended up feeling like she was on trial. Even Weidner's most innocuous questions seemed to catch her off-stride. When he referred to "the incident," she countered by calling it "the accident."

And Sally Coulthurst admitted that John Peel might be reluctant to talk to the authorities, considering that the topic of conversation would be Peel's involvement in marijuana sales. She also made concessions about Peel's reaction to news that Dean Moon was alive, noting that her own reaction had been close to shock.

When the issue turned to money, however, Weidner played cute. He never directly suggested that Sally Coulthurst's son sold drugs to make his boat payments. Instead, he drew attention to the $100,000 in unpaid fish tickets, in effect asking her to subtract it from Mark's net worth. He pointed out that another portion of the estate—$115,000 to be exact—was from the sale of Mark's fishing permits. By the time he was finished, he had whittled the estate down by at least a quarter million dollars. Mark Coulthurst, he seemed to be saying, had needed an extra source of money to make his payments.

On re-direct, Bob Blasco tried to undo Weidner's implications. He jumped on Peel's sale of marijuana to Dean Moon. He sneeringly referred to Peel's "dates" with Lisa Coulthurst, prompting Sally Coulthurst to say they had "dated occasionally." He guided her through easy questions about Mark's success as a fisherman, and then drilled in on Mark's advance payments on his boat loan.

"And based on everything you know about your son and his prior businesses," he asked, "do you have any doubt that he would have paid that loan off in accordance with the loan?"

"I have no doubt he would have paid it," she said. After everything that the defense had done to undermine her son's reputation, she only hoped the jury believed her.

29

As the last few days of the prosecution case fluttered on the horizon, Henry was left with one final witness. Jim Robinson. He was the man who had owned Craig Auto at the time of the *Investor* incident. The man who had looked at lineup photographs during the summer of 1984 and said, "I don't remember anything. I couldn't identify anybody anyway." Then something changed. He saw John Peel during a February 1986 hearing and identified him as the man who'd bought gas from him on the day of the fire. Robinson was prepared to go into court and do it again.

In a conference with Judge Schulz before Robinson's testimony, however, Henry asked what the judge thought was an unusual question. "What if Jim Robinson's name isn't Jim Robinson?" she asked. "Would that make a difference?" The judge said it wouldn't, but his curiosity was piqued. Soon enough, he would find out why Henry was being so coy.

In the courtroom, Henry had Robinson recall his fateful visit to Ketchikan Superior Court to testify at a Peel hearing. He'd sat in the back of the court because he wasn't immediately being called to testify.

"And then I came up on the stand and sat there for, I don't know how long it was, and I recognized a gas buyer," he said soberly.

"Now when you recognized the gas buyer at the time you were at this last hearing," Mary Anne Henry asked, "how sure were you of that?"

"Positive," Robinson replied.

"And do you see him in the courtroom today?" Henry asked.

"Yes, I do," he said.

"May the record reflect the identification of John Peel as the gas buyer," Henry triumphantly announced.

"It may," Judge Schulz responded. To himself, he was thinking something else. He was thinking, here is a man who had people coming in and out of his gas station. He's testifying that some guy he doesn't know and had never seen before came in and bought gas, then walked off. Now, two years later, he's saying he's absolutely positive John Peel was that guy. Schulz had "real doubts" as to the reliability of Robinson's testimony.

But Mary Anne Henry wasn't finished with Jim Robinson. She asked him why he was sure Peel was the person who bought gas. "I remember a face," Robinson asserted. "I don't hardly forget a face when I see one."

Phillip Weidner was keen on establishing reasonable doubt about Robinson's identification of John Peel. "You have said, now, that you're positive that Mr. Peel is the person that bought gas from you, correct?" Weidner inquired.

"Yes, I have," Robinson answered.

"You understand that there's a difference sometimes between being positive and correct?" Peel's attorney asked.

"I guess that may be possible," the man admitted.

After taking Robinson through a shopping list of things he didn't pay attention to when he saw the gas buyer—eyebrows, eyes, ears, chin, cheekbones, height and weight—Weidner asked about the subject's hair. Robinson claimed he must have paid attention to the hair, because he remembered the young man had bushy hair under his hat.

"Well, just on that point, sir, when you first talked to the troopers two days after the incident, you couldn't remember what the hair was, could you?" Weidner suggested.

"I don't recall, Mr. Weidner," Robinson replied, pronouncing it "Weedner." The defense attorney immediately took umbrage, much to the delight of the Coulthurst family sitting only a few rows back. "If you would be kind enough, my name is Weidner, sir," the attorney corrected.

"Weidner," Robinson repeated, as if trying out a new sound for the first time.

"I understand; it's a common error," Weidner added almost apologetically. "But…"

The defense attorney moved on, noting with some pleasure that the mechanic couldn't remember the gas buyer's hair only two days after the murder. "But by some miraculous process, now you say you can remember his hair, correct?" Weidner asked

"No, I think I told you, Mr. Weidner, before that…" Robinson again called the defense attorney "Weedner."

"If you would be kind enough, sir, the name is Weidner," the attorney corrected, again to the amusement of the Coulthurst's and others in the courtroom.

"Or Weidner," Robinson replied absent-mindedly.

Weidner immediately moved into an area of questioning that was to prove even more explosive. He started by asking Robinson to admit he'd had verbal conversations with a defense investigator. Robinson agreed he had. "Did you tell him you were going to make a deal with the prosecution because you were worried about charges Outside that your attorney was working on?" Weidner demanded.[17]

"No," Robinson insisted.

"You've had your attorney working on charges Outside, haven't you?" Weidner shot back.

Mary Henry hastily asked to approach the bench. Judge Schulz was about find out why she had been so coy. Jim Robinson was a fugitive from justice wanted on an escape charge in Arizona. Henry wanted a quick ruling: no questions about Robinson's past offenses, because they weren't relevant. Weidner thought they were relevant— he insisted Robinson had struck a deal with Henry's office. The judge ruled in Henry's favor—sort of. Weidner couldn't ask Robinson about his crimes, but could ask about conversations where he'd allegedly admitted his legal troubles.

When questioned, Robinson denied talking to anyone about wanting make a deal with the prosecution. He denied telling the defense investigator he couldn't talk to him because he was afraid of the prosecution and had to get things worked out "on charges Outside." He denied every one of Weidner's charges. Mary Anne Henry, meanwhile, successfully raised a blockade of objections.

---

17 "Outside" is Alaska-speak for the lower 48 states.

Finally, a frustrated Weidner requested a visit to the judge's chambers, where he complained that every question he wanted to ask about Robinson's past was being turned away. The judge ruled Weidner could attempt to establish bias by questioning Robinson closely about statements he'd allegedly made to the defense investigator. But the longest day belonged to Jim Robinson because, though ill with bladder cancer, passing blood in his urine and overdue for surgery, he had to return to testify the following day.

The next day was more of the same. Once more, Weidner honed in on Robinson's legal problems. The man denied that they worried him. He tried to get Robinson to admit there was a link between these legal problems and his sudden identification of John Peel. Between Henry's objections and Robinson's denials, nothing much came of it. Robinson said he never talked to his attorney about the possibility of being extradited and never had her make contacts with the prosecution.

The poignancy of the situation was not lost on the courtroom. Weidner had done much to damage Robinson's credibility. Henry decided to quit while she was ahead. She decided against calling her next scheduled witness, a Craig contractor who had allegedly identified John Peel. She acknowledged to reporters that she expected a number of problems to arise should the man be called to testify.

The Coulthurst's, meanwhile, had finally found something to chuckle about. From that time forward, they referred to John Peel's attorney as "Mr. Weedner."

30

Roy Tussing sat in an anteroom while he waited his turn to testify; he wanted to leave and never come back. The *Investor* dead had been fellow crewmembers. He owed them his voice. But he had also crewed with John Peel. What if Peel didn't do this and had been falsely accused? Didn't he owe John, too? Tussing didn't know what to think. He didn't know whether John was innocent or guilty. That tore at him.

Trying to calm himself, the fisherman everyone called "R. T." told himself to just go in and answer the questions truthfully. Yet he remained anxious. The reason was Phillip Weidner.

The prosecution tried hard to prepare him for cross-examination. They told him he had to be careful when he testified, lest the defense trick him into an answer he couldn't take back. They told him the defense could ask leading questions, that they could fudge the truth in an attempt to discredit him. From where Tussing sat, he imagined Phillip Weidner to be a "giant, rip your head off type of guy." Everyone, it seemed, was intimidated by him.

Tussing had no reason to doubt them and his worst fears were confirmed when he saw Ruth Moon during the break. Dean Moon's mother had preceded him to the witness stand. She was in tears by the time she was finished, and Tussing got the impression the defense had, "just torn her apart."

What finally kept Tussing from running was the realization that people were depending on him; he had information that they wanted to hear, or he wouldn't be there. When he walked into the courtroom shortly past 1:30, he had it in mind to do the right thing.

Inside the courtroom, Tussing felt another tug of emotion. He was not prepared for all the eyes staring at him. The thought that he would be asked possibly embarrassing questions in front of the jury once more impressed upon him the seriousness of his testimony. And then, from the witness stand, he caught a glance of John Peel. Peel seemed to be looking at him too, but neither man allowed their eyes to linger. Tussing's former crewmate instead looked down at the defense table, where he had a writing tablet.

In Mary Anne Henry's hands, Tussing drove down a road of personality profiles. Mark Coulthurst was "very ambitious, hard driving and fair." If a crewmember screwed up, Tussing said, he gave them a second, third or fourth chance. If there was a problem, Mark found a way to work around it. "He was pretty easy to get along with," Tussing said, "but he could be difficult to get along with." Sometimes, he added, Mark could rub people the wrong way.

John Peel, on the other hand, emerged as someone likable, but irresponsible. Tussing said he got along fine with Peel, but there was a "difference when it came to work habits." Peel was "less ambitious than the rest of us." And, Tussing said diplomatically, he didn't carry his load "as freely as other people did."

Despite Henry's relatively mild questions, Tussing could take little comfort. He still had to face Phillip Weidner. But when Weidner stood up and Tussing finally came face to face with the man, he realized something. Weidner was shorter than him. This giant of a man wasn't a giant. All of a sudden, Tussing wasn't so intimidated. As Peel's attorney moved into his questions, R. T. realized something else. Weidner was being nice to him.

Still, Tussing was too concerned about his performance to relax his guard. He ended up helping the defense as much as he helped the prosecution. In the opening minute of his testimony, for instance, R.T. said that he never noticed any hostility between Coulthurst and Peel. Tussing also confirmed that, in the days before he was fired, John Peel and others helped prevent *The Kit* from sinking in Bellingham harbor. And, he said, John Peel was easy-going and non-violent when he smoked marijuana or was drunk.

On redirect, Henry had only two questions of substance. The first was about Tussing's alleged concern as to how Mark Coulthurst was going to make his boat payments. Tussing answered that Coulthurst would have "worked harder." The second was about allegations that Mark Coulthurst was selling cocaine to make those boat payments.

"I'd say it wasn't true," R.T. said stolidly. "It's a lie. I mean, he would do it by fishing harder."

"Thank you, sir," Henry said. "I have no other questions."

As Roy Tussing walked out of the courtroom, he felt an abiding sense of relief. He was finished with this painful duty.[18] He was proud that he had answered everyone's questions, and not once tripped over himself. Mary Anne Henry, meanwhile, had turned to address Judge Schulz. Almost as an afterthought, she announced, "May it please the Court, the State rests."

An audible sigh of relief was heard from the spectators. That same sigh squeaked out of a few jurors. Judge Schulz was somewhat surprised—the state's case had ended with a whimper, not a bang. He suspected that they would have preferred to end with Jim Robinson pointing at John Peel, but everyone knew how that had turned out. At least now the end, while not yet in sight, was on the horizon. Schulz thought the case might end very soon.

"Don't be surprised," he told his law clerk, "if the defense rests when they come back in. When you stop and think about it, they can do themselves a lot of harm. But there's not a helluva lot more good they can do themselves that they haven't already done."

---

18 Few knew how difficult it was for Roy Tussing to testify. When he was six years old, his mother was murdered outside his bedroom window. Testifying in the *Investor* case brought those memories flooding back unbidden.

31

Phillip Weidner said the defense case might last as long as two months. He predicted it would take more like three or four weeks. But right out of the box, it was clear that the defense strategy was changing. After months of harping about drug money and professional killers, it became evident that the defense team was prepared to offer far less to the jury. The first hint of the shift came when Brant McGee said that they planned to prove Peel had an alibi for the night of the killings and that the prosecution was "in for some surprises."

The next day McGee and Weidner told reporters they would offer an "impossibility" defense, their point being that it was impossible for John Peel to have committed the crimes. They now would prove Peel's innocence, they said, through expert witnesses and the testimony of a "wide spectrum" of character witnesses. Weidner later elaborated on that theme, announcing that he planned to focus less on evidence pointing away from Peel and more on proving the prosecution couldn't hang the killings on him.

"There's a number of situations," Weidner proclaimed of the murders. "We do not know who killed them."

The cagey attorney was much more assured when it came to judging the state of the prosecution's case at this psychic and procedural boundary line. That assurance had clearly defined the shift in strategy. The state's case, Weidner declared, was "devoid of any real evidence," and was supportive of Peel's innocence when viewed in the proper light.

According to Weidner, prosecutors had failed to show any sign of hostility between John Peel and Mark Coulthurst, the presumed focus of the murderer. Continuing a favorite theme, Weidner again accused the prosecution of "twisting the truth" of witness testimony in the grand jury proceedings that had twice led to Peel's indictment.

Since neither side had ever missed an opportunity to posture or trade barbs, this time was no exception. Mary Anne Henry immediately hit back on Weidner's comments to reporters. To his charge that the state's case was devoid of evidence she replied, "I don't know where he has been for the past five months. I rested because I felt that there was sufficient evidence to find Peel guilty."

Henry was even more pointed in addressing the alleged lack of ill feeling between Peel and Coulthurst. "There is evidence of an underlying animosity that blew up on the night of the murders," she said. "The fact that John Peel wasn't exhibiting hostility to Mark Coulthurst every waking minute doesn't mean there wasn't underlying hostility."

Despite the rhetoric, there was one thing both sides agreed upon. Four years had passed since the crimes had been committed, and ferreting out alibis and incriminating statements from witnesses had gotten dicey at best. "Most witnesses' memories have dimmed somewhat," Henry conceded, "which makes it difficult to present the case in a cogent manner. I'd say that's been the major problem."

Weidner put it only slightly differently, saying that, "We've been handicapped by the tremendous amount of time between the crime and when he was arrested."

In Weidner's view, the police and prosecution had used that time to manipulate witness memories. One witness the state presumably hadn't manipulated was the first witness for the defense. This was the eyewitness who told of spotting a stocky, dark-complexioned, Native man boarding the *Investor* skiff. The day was Tuesday, the day the *Investor* burned. The time, he told the jury, was 45 minutes before the fire. The witness said the man "fiddled around for a few minutes," then untied the skiff's lines and left. He did not notice where he went.

With that background established, Weidner turned to John Peel and had him stand. Then he turned to the witness. He asked if Peel was the man he had seen clambering into the *Investor* skiff.

"No, it's not," the fisherman replied.

Mary Anne Henry attacked the man's credibility inside—and outside—the courtroom. Two days after the fire, the man told troopers he believed the sighting came two hours before the *Investor* blaze. The defense, Henry noted, "has now got him down to 45 minutes. They are inferring that the man he sighted is the guy who burned the *Investor*, when in fact he isn't."

But the defense was not banking its case entirely on witnesses that could contradict prosecution witnesses. There simply weren't enough witnesses available to refute each and every one of them. That's where the defense's array of experts came in. They matched the specialties of the prosecution's experts one-for-one, with a few toppers thrown in for good measure. A cynic might argue they were the best that money could buy, although they came despite the state's superior resources.

Weidner had already dispatched with the prosecution's FBI ballistics expert, Donald Reidman, grilling him about the uncertainties surrounding his identification of the murder weapon. Reidman's testimony was that Dean Moon's .223 was likely not the murder weapon, but he could only "absolutely eliminate" one weapon as the possible murder weapon, and that was a Marlin rifle found on the *Libby 8*. The bullet recovered from Mark Coulthurst's skull could have come from any one of thousands or millions of guns—*including* Larry Demmert's rifle found on the *Libby 8*. To be kind, this was not exactly "smoking gun" testimony.

Of all the prosecution experts, forensic dentist Dr. Gary Bell was perhaps the most important. Dean Moon was the hardest suspect to dismiss: his body had never been found. On examining the dental evidence, Bell had concluded it was "highly probable" that some of the teeth he examined belonged to Dean Moon.

The defense countered with a forensic dentist who seemed to have the better credentials. He was the chief forensic dentist for San Diego County and one of only 61 forensic dentists certified by the American Board of Forensic Odontology, of which he was former president. He worked with the FBI in bite mark and dental identification cases and held a Congressional appointment to the National Crime Information Center. As he got deeper into his testimony, however, Judge Schulz started to think him a prima donna.

Worse yet, to the judge's mind, he had not conducted his own tests. He had merely reviewed someone else's work—the state's dentist—and examined only five of the 21 teeth that had been found. Had it been a judge-tried case, Schulz would have disregarded his testimony as practically useless. That didn't stop the man from testifying.

"There's very definite doubt" Dean Moon died on the *Investor*, the witness told Weidner. In counterpoint, Gullufsen noted that two of the fire-scorched bicuspid roots found on the *Investor* had "pretty much the same curve" as Moon's pre-death x-ray.

"Pretty much doesn't cut it," the dentist replied scathingly. The dentist contended that no particle of dental remains thought to be from Dean Moon had any certainty of belonging to him. And while the defense expert refused to say the dental remains were from Moon, he conceded that he couldn't positively rule them out. That was a major concession, but Judge Schulz got the impression that no one on the jury had noticed.

The defense's next expert, meanwhile, openly contradicted the prosecution's arson expert. John Kennedy, a Chicago-based fire investigator, told jurors that the prosecution's expert was wrong when he testified about the accelerant used in the *Investor* fire.

But Kennedy had problems of his own. Prosecutors accused him of bilking Chubb and Son Insurance by submitting invoices for work he hadn't done. In a hearing before Judge Schulz, the man conceded he had kept $50,000 for two years, even though he hadn't conducted any fire investigations. In court papers filed in the fraud case, he was accused of creating false reports, a practice he denied. He said it was common practice for insurance companies to briefly retain a fire investigator to prevent them from testifying for the opposition.

Judge Schulz ruled that the witness' involvement in the fraud case lacked probative value. He said the prosecution hadn't proven that the man's reputation was questionable or that he had a bias against prosecutors. The prosecution, complaining that the judge's ruling had "handcuffed" them, said they now wouldn't bring up the subject of fraud. Schulz's restrictions, they said, made it impossible to accurately explain their accusations. Kennedy's assertions would stand, largely unchallenged.

32

When it came down to it, the prosecution had three, maybe four, witnesses who could put John Peel in incriminating places at incriminating times. Three of those witnesses had directly identified him in court. As the defense moved its case forward, it continued its attack on all three.

One of them, the Ruth Ann's waitress who served the Coulthurst's their last supper, was the sole woman in the trio. In the effort to undermine her credibility, the defense suggested she was a cocaine dealer. Judge Schulz turned them back. The defense then said her memory was faulty, using a nationally renowned memory expert, Dr. Elizabeth Loftus, to bolster their argument. Loftus argued that the woman had a tendency to "fill in the gaps" of her memory. She hadn't really seen John Peel with the Coulthurst's on the night of the murders, said Loftus. She had seen him in December of 1985, when the defense visited Craig to prepare for Peel's trial and distributed reward posters.

Target number two was Larry Demmert, Jr. Although the defense had worked him over for five days on the stand, they were not finished with him. His substance abuse and drinking, Weidner charged, had caused him to lose his memory of specific incidents. Not only that, Weidner insisted, Demmert may have been suffering from a medical phenomenon known as "confabulation." If he was, the attorney continued, he would fill in the gaps in his memory—there was that phrase again—with "memories that don't exist."

To determine if that was indeed the case, Weidner pushed Judge Schulz for access to Demmert's alcohol treatment records. He wanted a Kentucky pharmacologist, and reputed expert on the effects of alcohol, to examine those records for signs of confabulation. Short of that,

Weidner wanted the judge to force Demmert to meet with the defense pharmacologist. The defense strategy was plain. With the medical records and a favorable assessment, they could broaden their attack on Demmert to characterize him as a man whose "addled" brain was capable of creating false incriminatory recollections.

Within a week of the defense request, the judge ruled that he would not release Demmert's medical records to the defense. His ruling left the door open, or at least slightly ajar. Schulz told Weidner he could try to convince again him that Demmert's records should be released. Those documents never became part of the public record.

Their final target was Jim Robinson. Weidner was intent on proving the man had made a deal with the prosecution in return for favorable testimony. So intent that he issued two subpoenas—one for Robinson's lawyer, Trish Collins, and one for Mary Anne Henry.

Judge Schulz couldn't see how he could allow defense questioning of the contacts between Henry and Collins without violating attorney-client privilege. The very first question of Collins, he imagined, would attempt to establish whether she was Robinson's attorney—itself a violation of attorney-client privilege. In his ruling, he turned away the wide-ranging request. With that ruling, Judge Schulz avoided the prospect of the trial careening into ever more dangerous death spirals.

As it was, attention turned instead to questions of John Peel's character. That John Peel's character witnesses said good things about him was expected. Weidner intended to use Peel's release on bail as evidence that those close to him felt strongly about his innocence. There was no question that folks had rallied behind him. They used words like "polite," "hard-working" and "happy-go-lucky" to describe him.

"He was the most mellow kid you've ever seen," noted Peel neighbor Ruth Randmel.

"Why, he didn't even have the nerve to punch anyone," said her son, Bret. "He is the biggest chicken you've ever seen. When he got mad, he'd get red and walk off. I'd believe it was my mother before I'd believe it was him."

Within days of John Peel's arrest, several petitions had circulated in support of him. One gained 1,500 signatures within days; it requested the dismissal of murder charges against Peel and asked for his release on personal recognizance, "until such time that further substantial, untainted evidence is produced clearly linking John to the crime." A second petition circulated by family and friends contained a character witness statement that vouched "for John's credibility and good moral character." That petition included a demand that Peel be released on $1,000 bail.

But Pat Gullufsen argued for a close interpretation of the rules governing such witnesses. Those rules were clear. While the defense could call character witnesses, they could only testify to the reputation of the accused *at the time of the crime.* In a murder case, moreover, character testimony was limited to the defendant's reputation for peacefulness or non-violence. Peel's friends and family ended up saying far less than Weidner planned.

One of Peel's character witnesses was Charles Bertels, his father-in-law since 1981. Bertels hadn't spent as much time with Peel before 1982 as he had afterwards, but it didn't stop him from having opinions. His years with the Shore Patrol and as a juvenile corrections officer, he said, gave him the ability to know if a young man had violent tendencies.

"I cannot conceive of John Peel doing something violent," he said on the witness stand. "He's as laid back and mellow a boy as I've encountered."

Asked whether he would tell the jury Peel was violent, if that was what he believed, Bertels said he would. "John's wife is my daughter. I wouldn't do anything to cause her to spend the rest of her life with a man capable of doing the crimes he is charged with."

Gullufsen had only two questions for Charles Bertels. *Was in he in Craig on the night of the murders? And if so, did he see John Peel there?* No, the father-in-law answered, he wasn't there. And no, he didn't see him.

And so it went for the entire cast of character witnesses. The only one of any substance was John Peel's wife, and *only* because she was his wife; Ruth Moon knew well the impact Cathy Peel had in the courtroom and said as much. "John Peel and his wife and his sister and his baby are [there] and my son is six feet under," Moon told the *Bellingham Herald.* "If I were brave enough, I'd like to take a big picture of my son and hold it [in court]. It is a chance to say, 'this is one of eight people who are gone.' "

Cathy Peel's appearance was brief and came only after Phillip Weidner managed to severely limit the scope of her testimony. She answered a few background questions about her marriage and her child with John. She said she received a wedding present from Mark and Irene Coulthurst, which she identified in a soft voice as, "silver plated hurricane candlesticks." The card that came with the gift, she said, had been lost. With that, Weidner announced that he had "nothing further" to ask John Peel's wife. Her testimony ended so abruptly that several jurors were seen exchanging questioning glances.

If Phillip Weidner lost momentum with the curious non-testimony of Cathy Peel, he quickly regained it with his next two witnesses. One, a Craig First Bank vice president, testified that John Peel had purchased $1,000 worth of traveler's checks on the day of the fire. The transaction, the bank officer said, occurred sometime between 3:00 p.m. and 5:00 p.m. on September 7, 1982. There was no way, he added, to determine the exact time of the transaction. But, he testified, the process of obtaining the checks would have taken five to ten minutes.

The other witness was a Craig resident who deposited church funds at the bank just before Peel purchased his traveler's checks. She remembered watching smoke from the *Investor* fire for approximately five minutes—and told the jury that she "probably" ventured to the bank after that. She said it was her habit to make the deposit on Tuesdays—the fire occurred on a Tuesday—after picking up her son from school at 2:50 p.m.

Outside court, Weidner reminded reporters that testimony had already established the *Investor* skiffman did not reach the cold storage dock until after 4:40 p.m. Weidner was firm in his conviction that it would have been impossible for Peel to set the *Investor* fire, race into Craig, buy traveler's checks and make a 4:49 p.m. phone call. "Sooner or later the prosecution is going to have to face reality," he insisted. "And this is another dose of reality for them. I'm sure they will react to this with anger and scorn."

The uncertainty about the timing of Peel's bank visit, however, left Weidner's assertions open to criticism. Mary Anne Henry characterized them as "just more ink the squid spills into the water" to cloud the impressions of the jury. John Peel, she said, likely purchased the traveler's checks before the fire—an assertion consistent with the church clerk's 3:00 p.m. banking habit—and the Craig resident probably saw the smoke after leaving the bank.

Weidner seemed little worried about the discrepancies. The bank testimony fit into his larger theme of official incompetence. To underscore that point, he immediately followed the travelers check testimony with a defense expert who pointed to the state's failure to obtain fingerprint evidence—another sign of a bungled investigation.

The expert was George Bonebrake, a retired 34-year veteran of the FBI's Latent Fingerprint Section and the man who had identified James Earl Ray's fingerprint on the rifle used to kill Dr. Martin Luther King, Jr. Bonebrake insisted that troopers should have tried to take prints from the *Investor* skiff on the day after the fire, saying that the rainfall that day wouldn't have washed away fingerprints made by an arsonist's fuel-soaked hands.

To Schulz's mind, the state had missed a trick by not having their own fingerprint expert. Better to call in a fingerprint expert to testify that they'd found nothing than to have no expert at all.

33

Ketchikan, Alaska
August 7, 1986

The controversy surrounding Jim Robinson would not die. Phil Weidner wouldn't let it. The defense suspicion that the former owner of Craig Auto had struck a deal with the prosecution had grown as they dug deeper into his past. A background check on the man, using the name Robinson, turned up nothing.

But the defense had turned up a witness who told of a conversation she'd had with the woman who was now Robinson's wife. Charlotte Robinson tearfully told a friend on the eve of her marriage that she believed her fiancée was using a false name and his mother's social security number. Charlotte Robinson also told her friend that she thought her husband's actual last name was Robertson. Weidner was now certain the man was using an alias—which prompted charges that he had perjured himself when he told jurors his name was Jim Robinson.

At the center of these allegations was an eight-year-old crime Robinson had committed in Arizona. As Robinson's identity became known, everyone seemed to know the nature of that crime—except the jury. Weidner set out to correct that discrepancy, charging that Robinson's refusal to answer questions about his past hindered the defense from exploring allegations of bias toward the prosecution. It wasn't the first time Weidner had asked for full discovery in the matter. This time, Judge Schulz agreed and, hoping that Robinson would shed some light on his past, ordered a hearing outside the jury's presence.

When Jim Robinson took the witness stand he was tight-faced

and tight-lipped. He looked often toward his attorney, Tricia Collins, for guidance. Phillip Weidner, meanwhile, steadfastly refused to call Robinson by name, instead calling him "sir," or referring to him in the third person as "whoever he is."

"What is your true name?" Weidner asked in his opening parry.

"I refuse to answer on the grounds that it may incriminate me and on Fifth Amendment rights of the Constitution," Robinson answered without emotion.

"Are there pending criminal charges in another state against you?" Weidner wondered.

"I refuse to answer on the grounds that it may incriminate me and on Fifth Amendment rights of the Constitution," Robinson answered again.

Weidner asked Robinson his date of birth and Social Security number—to no avail—then asked a series of questions that moved the subject closer to the nature of Robinson's past. Was he worried when he identified John Peel as the gas buyer that he might be extradited to Arizona? Had he fled the state to avoid prosecution?

As the hearing proceeded, Weidner dug deeper—so deep that Tricia Collins moved from the counsel table to the empty jury box, which put her at Robinson's elbow and allowed them to whisper between questions. More often than not, Robinson looked at his attorney before venturing a reply. Weidner, it seemed, was moving in for the kill.

"Did you apply explosives or fire to any car in Arizona?" he asked. Robinson took the Fifth.

"Did you firebomb a car in Arizona?" Weidner wanted to know. "Did you flee Arizona to avoid prosecution for firebombing a car or using an explosive device to damage a car in Arizona?"

There was more.

"Were you ever charged in any state with firebombing or using an explosive device?" Time and again, Weidner got the same reply. Robinson was in no mood for talking. He took the Fifth Amendment more than forty times during the hearing.

Neither side left the hearing with a decision—nor did Judge Schulz set a date for his ruling. Schulz wanted more information and knew he had to get it from Tricia Collins. Until the judge talked to Collins, the mystery of Jim Robinson was going to stay a mystery.

What Judge Schulz found out was that Jim Robinson was no innocent. His given name was Kenneth Harvey Robertson. He had a checkered past, including a 1973 charge of possessing a loaded shotgun and carrying a concealed weapon, for which he had served sixty months' probation. On August 29, 1979, he had torched a 1976 Chevrolet Monte Carlo parked outside an apartment building in Tucson, Arizona. The car belonged to a man with whom Robertson's estranged wife was having an affair.

Sentenced to four years in jail on the arson charge, Robinson was soon transferred into a work-release program. Four months from finishing his work release, he walked. That walk had eventually landed him in Craig, Alaska, where another, more serious, arson loomed on the horizon.

Judge Schulz ordered Robinson to be fingerprinted for an FBI check on his identity. He also ruled that the defense could call Robinson's wife to the stand if Robinson continued to avoid defense questions about his identity. Jim Robinson was suddenly faced with a difficult choice. He could either waive his Fifth Amendment right or expose his wife to Weidner's questions. Rather than let Weidner "humiliate my wife," as he put it, he chose the former course.

When Jim Robinson took the stand on August 7th, Phillip Weidner was more than ready. His approach was reminiscent of the one he had used with Larry Demmert, Jr. The defense attorney was piercing, relentless and on the attack from his very first question.

"You, sir, are a liar, is that correct?" Weidner asked.

"On what basis are you…" Robinson sputtered, stunned.

"Well, you've been lying for years about your true name, haven't you?"

"No," Robinson replied, regaining his composure. "I would like to explain that, if possible." During the course of his testimony, Robinson would repeatedly try to explain. But for the moment, Weidner wasn't going to let him.

"Well, first of all," the defense attorney demanded, "could you tell me yes or no? Have you been lying for years about your true name?"

"I would like to explain it," Robinson said again.

"Have you, or not, been lying for years about your true name?" Weidner demanded.

"My name is Jim Robinson," the witness insisted. Then he hedged. "My true name on my birth certificate is Kenneth Harvey Robertson."

In the end, Weidner was left with accusations that the prosecution had taken a "hear no evil, see no evil" approach to Robinson's troubles. All the state wanted, he suggested, was for Robinson to come in "and finger Mr. Peel," no questions asked. And wasn't it curious, he added, that these were the same prosecutors who'd been willing to spend $30,000 on models and hundreds of thousands of dollars on the rest of their investigation.

"No, that's not what went on, Mr. Weidner," Jim Robinson quietly replied. "Obviously, I wouldn't have had the problems I had if I wouldn't have been here."

Phillip Paul Weidner had reached the end of the road with the former owner of Craig Auto. In chambers, he told the court that he was still investigating Jim Robinson, and wanted to preserve his right to bring the witness back to the stand "in the event of new discovery on this matter."

When the attorneys returned to the courtroom, Weidner announced that he had no further questions for Jim Robinson. Judge Schulz told the witness he could step down.

And then, without fanfare, without emotion, without the sense of drama for which he had become well known, Phillip Paul Weidner calmly said, "Your Honor, based on the state of the record the defense, at this time, would rest its case."

The defense case ended much like the prosecution's: it hadn't so much ended as it had stopped, like it had run out of breath. Notable too was that none of the so-called cocaine conspiracy witnesses were called. That would have been too much of a good thing.

34

Ketchikan, Alaska
Tuesday, August 19 - Friday, August 22, 1986

After eight months and more than two million dollars, closing arguments in Alaska's longest-running criminal trial were set to begin. As had often been the case, the presentations to the jury didn't begin before another round of fighting between the prosecution and defense. Mary Anne Henry filed several motions, one of which sought to prohibit Peel's lawyers from referring to any of 39 topics during closing statements.

Among the statements Henry sought to ban were references to drug dealing by Mark Coulthurst. After winning a partial victory— Judge Schulz banned drug references and six other topics—there was nothing left but the speeches.

The point man for the prosecution was Pat Gullufsen and, by tradition, he went first. Gullufsen had emerged as the steadiest player on the state's team, so the honor was fitting, if somewhat ironic. Mary Anne Henry hadn't always seemed overjoyed about his presence, and now he was giving the state's final argument. Gullufsen's challenge was formidable: he had to summarize eight months of intricate, often contradictory, testimony without confusing the jury or making its task more difficult than it already was.

The courtroom, which was often less than full during the course of the trial, was packed as Gullufsen began. He opened with a concession to reality. "We may never know what happened on the *Investor*, who was shot where or who fell first or the sequence of steps that were taken," he noted in his resonant baritone. "But what you will know is that John Peel is the murderer."

"You won't get all the way into his head," Gullufsen suggested, "but you will get far enough to see why, and there will be some clues to tell us how."

Gullufsen scoffed at Weidner's recurring theories as to the cause of the murders. There was no evidence that the killings had been carried out by professional hit men, gangster killers, drug assassins or "strangers in the night," Gullufsen asserted. "There's only John Peel."

Absent any plot to kill the *Investor* crew, the evidence pointed to what Gullufsen called the "survival steps" taken by John Peel in the hours and days after the murders. He said Peel had to move the *Investor* to Ben's Cove after the killings, because his nervousness would have caused him to "stand out like a blinking light in the dark." He went on to suggest that Peel returned to burn the boat the following day because he had left a tin of marijuana on board. That tin, Gullufsen declared, "spelled" John Peel—and would have led authorities to him had it been found on the *Investor*. But Peel was not as cool a customer as people might think, Gullufsen suggested.

"He was certainly in shock" after committing the murders, Gullufsen said, "but he is not a master-minded criminal who has this all planned out."

Gullufsen harkened back to the many witnesses they had brought to the stand. He began with Dawn Holmstrom—who he called a liar. She had lied, he said, by telling police John Peel was with her in downtown Craig when she knew he wasn't. Yet even if Dawn Holmstrom was a liar, Gullufsen wanted the jury to believe at least one of her statements. He pointed to her grand jury recitation of John Peel's confession, in which she reported that Peel had said, "It all happened so fast, I can't believe I did it."

Gullufsen also reminded jurors of the "alarming" statement that John Peel had made to Brian Polinkus on the day of the fire, when he speculated that Mark Coulthurst may have "tweaked out and killed everyone." Gullufsen added that Polinkus had told a Bellingham friend he suspected Peel was responsible for the crimes.

"He never would have said that unless he knew some pretty specific things," Gullufsen suggested.

Larry Demmert, meanwhile, had spent nine days on the witness stand because he was, in Gullufsen's words, at the "wrong place at the wrong time." Demmert's bad timing had led him to see John Peel on a North Cove dock, holding a rifle, just after the murders. Addressing Weidner's assertion that Peel's former skipper had conveniently failed to report his sighting of Peel until the day of the grand jury, Gullufsen said Demmert kept his mouth shut because he didn't want to "become the one who is finking on John Peel."

And what of Weidner's claim that Demmert had invented the sighting out of a combination of Valium addiction and police pressure? Those theories, Gullufsen said, were untrue. Instead, the assistant prosecutor asserted, Demmert went to doctors seeking Valium because his knowledge of the crimes caused him considerable anxiety.

While Gullufsen addressed the jury, John Peel stayed busy in his usual fashion—by writing notes on a yellow legal pad. When the prosecutor glared at him, Peel stared back. His chief attorney, meanwhile, managed to raise several objections—when he wasn't yawning. After four hours of addressing the jury, Gullufsen had the good sense to call a recess. He would finish his remarks, he said, the following morning.

Outside court, Weidner called Gullufsen's remarks "speculation and conjecture," adding that "you can tell a good story, but courts and juries require evidence." Weidner's partner, the often-silent Michael Tario, was less kind. He called Gullufsen's closing argument, "long, boring and tedious." He also suggested that it had "put the jury to sleep."

Judge Schulz, for one, disagreed. He had noticed that the jury couldn't keep their eyes off Pat Gullufsen.

When Gullufsen returned to court the following morning, he presented a detailed scenario of that deadly night on board the *Investor*. The precipitating incident, Gullufsen speculated, occurred when John Peel visited Mark Coulthurst at Ruth Ann's restaurant on the night of the killings. Peel, bold as always, had asked his former skipper for a job. The *Investor*, after all, was down one crewman—LeRoy Flammang had left the boat and returned to Blaine. Mark Coulthurst had turned him away.

After the turndown, Gullufsen said, John Peel left the restaurant and ended up back on the *Investor*. Once there, he smoked pot with crewmen Dean Moon and Jerome Keown. The dope smoking may have caused Mark Coulthurst, whom Gullufsen acknowledged could be caustic and insulting, to awaken. And when he saw Peel, the *Investor* skipper tossed him off his boat.

Peel came back and, when he returned, he was armed and angry. He wanted to "redeem himself," Gullufsen said, and confronted Mark Coulthurst. Seeing John Peel with a weapon, however, only succeeded in making Coulthurst irate. "The shots started and Mark is the first one to get shot," the prosecutor speculated. "Maybe Dean was next, trying to get up and do something, and Jerome next, because he was coming out of the bathroom."

"Irene starts screaming," Gullufsen continued, "and the only way to stop the screaming is to shoot where the screaming is coming from."

Investor crewmen Michael Stewart and Chris Heyman, meanwhile, lay quivering in the fo'c's'le. They were "hoping that whatever is out in the galley doesn't come through the door," Gullufsen said. "But it does come through the door."

After that, the only living souls on board were the Coulthurst children, whom the prosecutor suggested were killed by suffocation or blows to the head. Minutes later, Gullufsen concluded, Larry Demmert looked out the window of the *Libby 8*. Standing on the dock was John Peel. He was holding a rifle. There it was: the so-called smoking gun. In the prosecution's mind, it definitively established John Peel as the killer.

Phillip Paul Weidner was not about to be upstaged by Pat Gullufsen. When he took his place in front of the jury, he cautioned them not to be "swept away by fear" or listen to speculation and conjecture.

"We are commending the life of John Kenneth Peel to you," he noted as he began his closing arguments. In a bit of theatrics, he produced a blown-up photograph of the jury instruction on reasonable doubt. Holding it inches from Gullufsen' s face, he asked, "Would you rely on Larry Demmert if your life was at stake?"

Weidner also addressed three of the jurors by name, a tactic that drew an angry protest from Mary Anne Henry. According to at least one court opinion, she noted, the practice was considered "reprehensible."

Judge Schulz agreed. He told the attorney that addressing jurors was improper and told him not to do it again.

Equally interesting was Weidner's next foray, during which he defended John Peel's apparent evasions and lies to police. Peel neglected to tell police he had sold marijuana to Dean Moon and Jerome Keown, the defense attorney said, because he was afraid of incriminating himself and his wife Cathy, who had sent it to him by mail. Had he known he would become a murder suspect, Weidner suggested, John Peel would have been more forthright. Weidner added that Peel lied about going out to see the burning *Investor* because he was in a Craig bar at the time, selling marijuana.

Weidner also attacked the prosecution for suggesting that Dawn Holmstrom and Brian Polinkus were protecting John Peel. The state, he suggested, would have the jury believe that Peel's two crewmates were "gangsters and thugs who came in to cover up for a murderer." While he was at it, Peel's attorney also challenged the state's view that Peel had provided suspicious answers to police allegations he had committed the murders.

"There has to be a magic answer," he told the jury, suggesting there was no way Peel could have met police expectations.

Outside court, Weidner went further. He told reporters that his son, who had been in the courtroom, had an apt description of Pat Gullufsen's remarks earlier that day. "He said that the prosecutor is up there telling stories," Weidner noted. "It's a good story," he added. "And if we were talking about the boogie man and not about evidence, he'd win."

The following day witnessed a one-two punch by Weidner and Brant McGee. McGee made much of the failure of eyewitnesses to positively identify John Peel as the skiffman. Instead, they had said that John Peel "closely resembled" the skiffman.

"There is no doubt in my mind that the person in the skiff looks similar to John Peel," McGee conceded. "But does that mean he is the person? Either you are or you aren't," he said. "It's that simple."

McGee also referred to Dawn Holmstrom's grand jury testimony concerning John Peel's confession. "How could she come up with a statement that didn't happen?" he asked. "I know you wouldn't do that, and I know I wouldn't do that. But Dawn Holmstrom doesn't have the same equipment as you and I."

When Weidner took over, he went after the remaining prosecution witnesses, one by one. Of Larry Demmert he said, "The man is not worthy of belief. You can't rely on him beyond a reasonable doubt." Weidner's next target was Jim Robinson. Although Robinson had pointed an accusing finger at his client, Weidner had little to say about him. What he did say was pointed.

"I've practiced law long enough," he said, "that I can smell a rat."

Moving to Dean Moon, Weidner suggested there was no proof Moon had died aboard the *Investor*. And, he continued, "What one person in the world would want confusion about the bodies on the boat?" Weidner answered his own question. "Dean Moon," he replied. As Weidner spoke, Dean Moon's mother ran from the courtroom, grasping a handkerchief, tears streaming from her eyes.

Defying the judge's orders, Weidner also repeated a favorite refrain. He told jurors that the possibility cocaine was involved in the *Investor* murders was "something to consider." He further suggested that Mark Coulthurst was laundering drug money.

His character assassinations complete, Weidner ended his closing arguments with a self-penned bit of doggerel entitled, "To The Jury." In his best orator's voice, Weidner presented the jury with John Peel's final plea:

> Let your minds and hearts unite
> Help us in our hour of need
> All we ask
> Do what is right
> Justice lives within your being.

Mary Anne Henry, for one, wasn't impressed by the poem. After Weidner finished, she demanded that the defense lawyer be held in contempt for violating seven court orders restricting what could be discussed during summation. Judge Schulz said later that Weidner appeared to have violated six of those orders, but wouldn't rule until after the jury reached its decision.

The last word, as always, belonged to the state. Pat Gullufsen spent much of his time attacking Peel's alibis, which he portrayed as flimsy at best. Peel's purchase of traveler's checks, he said, did not eliminate the possibility that he set the *Investor* on fire. Gullufsen also lambasted the defense claim that Peel lied about his visit to the burning *Investor* because he was involved in a drug transaction.

"I've got two words for that one," Gullufsen as he grabbed a large piece of drawing paper. "Come On," he wrote in red ink.

A short while later, the stolid prosecutor turned his wrath to the man sitting at the center of their case. While not a theatrical lawyer, Gullufsen rose to the occasion. He pointedly directed the jury's attention toward John Peel. He reminded them why they were there.

"Keep looking at Mr. Peel," he told them, "because the evidence puts blood on his hands. The blood of Irene, Mark, Kimberly, John, Chris, Jerome, Mike and Dean Moon." Gullufsen paused, and then uttered his final sentence. "He's not going to reach the door with that blood on his hands."

With those remarks, Pat Gullufsen closed the book on the *Investor* murder case. Eight months of bickering were finally at an end. There was nothing more the lawyers could do. Within days, the jury would be sequestered and deliberating over John Peel's fate.

35

The jury had been sequestered at a Super 8 Motel since Thursday, August 21st, one day before closing arguments ended. On Saturday morning, August 23rd, a bus brought them to the State Office Building, where deliberations began in the jury room of Superior Court. Their number had been reduced to twelve, the legal minimum. Since neither side would agree to a verdict reached by a jury of eleven, the die was set. If one of the jurors could not continue, for whatever reason, the *Investor* case would automatically end in a mistrial.

As deliberations began, John Peel faced one of several fates. If the jury found him guilty of all eight murder charges and the arson, he faced up to eight hundred years in prison. If they found him not guilty—or couldn't find him guilty beyond a reasonable doubt—they could set him free. One thing they couldn't do was find him guilty of lesser charges. Although the prosecution had offered an instruction allowing the jury to reduce the charges if they found Peel had committed all or some of the murders without a "conscious objective" to kill, Judge Schulz rejected the proposal. He feared a compromise verdict.

"The way this case has been tried was 'he did it,' 'I didn't do it,' " Schulz commented in handing down his ruling. "And that's the way I'm going to do it."

The first three days of deliberations passed without incident. As the jury reached day four, it appeared they were wrestling with some of the evidence; that impression was reinforced by their request to hear the taped testimony of two witnesses who had seen the skiff operator. One of those witnesses was Sue Domenowske-Page.

Weidner protested the jury request, because they chose not

to listen to all of his cross-examination. Schulz pushed it aside and the jurors filed into the courtroom to hear the tapes replayed. Later that day, they sent the judge a note. In it they asked if witnesses were prohibited from making a positive identification of a defendant at trial. After much haggling over how to word the response, Schulz decided a simple "no" would suffice.

On day five, the jury asked for the trial transcripts of several key witnesses. Their request was turned down after Phil Weidner refused to stipulate to their accuracy. Once again the jury heard taped testimony. Who they heard said much about what they were thinking.

On their list was Joe Weiss, who testified for the state that he'd seen the skiffman in the *Investor* on the Monday before the fire. Also on the list was the man who had testified for the prosecution that he'd seen an Alaska Native man in the *Investor* skiff at about 2:30 p.m. on the day of the fire. The final person on the list was the state witness who had testified to seeing a man take a skiff out to the *Investor* at 3:50 p.m. on the day of the fire.

On day six, the jury returned to the courthouse at 8:30 a.m., starting their deliberations even earlier than Judge Schulz had recommended. At 2:10 p.m., they sent another note to Judge Schulz. This note said they were, "unable to reach a unanimous verdict." The judge immediately called in the attorneys for both sides; court watchers knew something was up when the attorneys conferred in chambers before going into the courtroom to hear the jury's response.

When the opposing sides returned to the open courtroom, both asked that the judge poll the jury. "It could very well avoid what might be a fruitless retrial," Weidner insisted. "If this jury is eleven to one for acquittal, there won't be a retrial. We should know that."

Judge Schulz refused the request.

Mary Anne Henry, meanwhile, asked that the jury be sent back to deliberate. The judge, she added, should repeat one of his final instructions before doing so. That instruction requested that jurors "not hesitate to reexamine" their positions, while reminding them not to "surrender an honest conviction for the mere purpose of returning a verdict."

Phillip Weidner protested Henry's request. "The state simply wants to coerce a verdict from the minority," he said. Instead, Weidner urged

Schulz to declare a mistrial. Schulz demurred, saying he first wanted to hear how long the jury had been deadlocked.

"If they've been in the same position for a day and a half, I'm going to be satisfied," the judge declared. "If they've taken one vote, I'm not."

The responsibility for answering Judge Schulz's question fell on the shoulders of Heidi Eckstrand, jury foreman and managing editor of the *Ketchikan Daily News*. As Schulz looked in her direction, his glasses were perched halfway down his nose. What he wanted to know, he told her, "[is] how long it's been since there's been any movement?"

Eckstrand rested her hand on her chin and pondered the Judge's question. She took a long moment before answering. "There has been some movement," she said thoughtfully. "I would say the last was this afternoon." But Eckstrand admitted they could get no further.

Schulz hesitated, his face solemn and serious. Finally he declared to jurors, "I'm going to discharge you. Words can't express my thanks," he added. "If you're satisfied you can't reach a verdict, I'll discharge you with our thanks." Before the jury left, however, Schulz had one more piece of business. "What happened in the jury room stays there," he said, as he ordered them to keep silent about their deliberations.

By 3:45 p.m. the jurors had left the courtroom, smiling and laughing while they hugged each other and the bailiff who had been their den mother. As they left the room, Phillip Weidner reached over and put his arm around his client. John Peel was heard to whisper "finally" as he jury left the room. With the jury gone, Judge Schulz declared the case a mistrial.

"I'm satisfied they were deadlocked and further deliberations wouldn't do any good," he told attorneys. "They gave it a good shot."

Minutes later, Weidner asked the judge to acquit his client. Such requests are routine at the end of trials, and Schulz immediately scheduled a hearing for the defense motion. He also tentatively declared that a second trial begin on January 20, 1987.

But of all decisions, a mistrial was the one guaranteed to please no one. Judge Schulz was particularly displeased, declaring outside the courtroom that, "the system didn't work. We didn't get a verdict and I'm disappointed." Yet Schulz was also concerned that further deliberations would have been fruitless. "I was satisfied by looking at the situation that it wouldn't do much good to send them out for another day," he said. "And that's still my position."

Family reactions to the end of the Peel trial were less than sanguine. Sally Coulthurst said she believed Peel was guilty and should face another trial. "I'm not particularly happy about it, but I don't want it stopped," she declared, referring to the prospect of a retrial. She added that a hung jury was "one step above a not-guilty verdict," but somehow would have preferred the latter. A not-guilty verdict, she said, would have at least put an end to the waiting game. "I would have learned to live with it," she said.

The fact that daughter Lisa was expecting a baby only complicated her feelings. "We're excited about having the baby," Sally Coulthurst said, "but nothing erases the loss of the others."

Ruth Moon was not so gracious. She openly criticized Schulz for letting the jury go. "Why in hell didn't they deliberate longer?" she asked. "They went seven months; why not take two more days? I realize that the jurors were tired, but why not let them take a nap and get back to it? It's too important a decision to make in such a short period of time."

If there was any comfort for Moon, it was that, "they didn't find John Peel not guilty. I hope he realizes that. He's not a free man as far as I'm concerned. I think it's a lousy deal," she added angrily. "I just know he is the guy."

The Peel family wasn't doing much better, although Phillip Weidner had thrust himself between them and waiting reporters, saying the family didn't want to comment. "It's too private a moment," he said. As John Peel left the courtroom, however, he commented to a photographer, "It could have been worse."

The only person who seemed at ease with the outcome was Phillip Paul Weidner. He had been buoyed by his observations of the jury as they listened to taped testimony. Their reactions, he said, gave him "a firm conviction that the majority of the jurors were on our side." He added that the mistrial was "irrefutable proof" that the state spent more than $1 million to prosecute an innocent man.

"Anyone could clearly recognize that that is a victory," Weidner added. "The bottom line is, no fair jury would ever convict John Peel. We had a fair jury in this case." Speaking on behalf of his client,

Weidner added that John Peel was "somewhat frustrated at not being totally vindicated."

Brant McGee, meanwhile, declared he was contemplating having the Alaska Department of Law "conduct an objective, independent review of the evidence before any decision is made to continue with this prosecution."

Mary Anne Henry scoffed at McGee's proposal, saying there was "sufficient evidence to find John Peel guilty of murder beyond a reasonable doubt." Indeed, within moments of the mistrial decision Henry contacted State Attorney General Hal Brown to inform him of her decision. "Without hesitation," she told reporters, "it's worthwhile to retry the case."

36

While Hal Brown worked on his retrial decision, Judge Schulz plowed forward. Phillip Weidner had already filed a number of motions, one asking to postpone the trial from January 1987 to December 1987, another to allow John Peel to get a job and move out of his parent's house. Would he request a change of venue? At a November 28th, 1986, hearing to answer these questions, Mary Anne Henry stepped into Judge Schulz' courtroom and surprised almost everyone.

"Your Honor," she said, her voice charged with emotion, "[a] matter was brought to my attention three days ago that requires the state as part of its ethical responsibility to pursue, both factually and legally. And until that matter is resolved, it is the state's position that no procedural or substantive issues can be resolved by this court in this case."

The mystery issue, Schulz soon found out, was that Phillip Weidner had been romantically linked to Cammy Oechsli, the judge's law clerk or, more accurately, his former law clerk. Word on the street was that they were lovers. To complicate matters, Oechsli had only recently left her position as Schulz's clerk. To confound things even more, she had just taken a new job with the Ketchikan Public Defender's office—the same entity that provided John Peel's co-counsel, Brant McGee.

In a motion to the court, Mary Anne Henry demanded that Judge Schulz remove himself from the Peel case. Failing that, she wanted Schulz disqualified. The Oechsli-Weidner romance was, to her mind, unethical. Given the nature of their relationship, Henry was convinced that Weidner now had an unfair advantage. Cammy Oechsli had no doubt delivered him Judge Schulz's every thought and attitude about the case.

Equally damning, from Henry's point of view, Oechsli had dated one of the defense investigators when they lived in Petersburg—and a second defense investigator was a former law school classmate and friend of Oechsli's.

Henry's motion detailed a host of other charges against Oechsli, which Henry insisted made it impossible for Schulz to continue with the Peel case. Henry charged, for instance, that Schulz had ordered the bank to produce John Peel's bank records, and told the bank not to discuss those records with the prosecution. Henry also raised questions about Schulz's failure to inform the state of Oechsli's relationship with Weidner, especially since Oechsli was a "potential witness in this matter."

During the first trial, it seemed, one of the defense experts had directly contacted Cammy Oechsli about the tape of John Peel's Bellingham police interview. The defense was charging that it had been altered, and their expert's job was to prove them right. Indeed, they had gone so far as to request the tape recorder troopers had used during the interview. The mere fact that Oechsli had talked to the defense expert, however, had given the defense cause to subpoena her for the second trial—even though Judge Schulz told the expert that direct contact with an officer of the court was a no-no, and to make future inquiries through the attorneys.

The Schulz-Weidner-Oechsli revelations hit a deep nerve with Mary Anne Henry. She was not Judge Schulz' biggest fan; it was her view that Schulz was the primary reason that one-in-twenty Ketchikan indictments were dismissed—the highest ratio in the state. "It's easier for him to find technicalities to dismiss," Henry claimed; that assessment was confirmed, in her mind, when the judge dismissed the first Peel indictment. Equally galling were the Schulz rulings that went against the prosecution—including his decision to exclude the "off the record" portions of John Peel's Bellingham police interview.

Phillip Weidner was himself another major source of conflict. Henry felt very much his equal and had the record to prove it: by her own estimate, she'd prosecuted up to thirty homicide cases, with only three defendants acquitted. It didn't seem to matter; in the courtroom, the two of them fought like name-calling school kids.

"I've noticed a change in Phil," Henry told reporters. "He has gotten a lot dirtier. And Brant McGee has too since the last time I had a trial with him. I don't know if it's this case, or just in general, or both."

It was here that Mary Anne Henry's Catholic sense of right and wrong—and her Jesuit education at Creighton University—came to the fore. Early on, she decided that she disliked defense work. "I had clients lie to me, and not show up, and get a good deal and screw it up in a month," she admitted, adding that she preferred representing victims and police officers.

"I feel I'm accomplishing something that can be measured every day," she said of her career as a prosecutor. "In major cases, society's rules are affirmed."

In that context, anything that gave Phillip Weidner a perceived advantage was anathema.

When news of the state's effort to remove him reached Schulz, meanwhile, he was hurt and angry. He knew the prosecution was unhappy about some of his decisions, but he didn't know they were that unhappy. He didn't see that he had done anything unethical, or that his objectivity had been compromised. He had not communicated any private thoughts to Cammy Oechsli, he told himself, because he had no private thoughts to share. He had laid everything out in public.

While Judge Schulz weighed his response to the prosecution demand, Phillip Weidner moved in with an opinion of his own. The prosecution, Weidner charged in a memorandum opposing Schulz's removal, was engaged in a "bad faith attempt at judge shopping."

"It is apparent that the prosecution, frustrated by the results of the jury vote, now hopes to retry Mr. Peel before another judge and hopes to obtain rulings more favorable to the prosecution, since they realize there is no good faith appellate court action that will change the proper rulings of the Court in the first trial."

The defense attorney also pointed out some apparent inconsistencies in Henry's application of the ethical canons. He noted that Mary Anne had no qualms about serving as lead prosecutor in cases where she had a "close personal relationship" with the police officers involved. "This includes," Weidner added, "the instant case in which Officer Glass was called as a material witness for the State and actually examined by Ms. Henry. Query as to whether Ms. Henry will excuse herself from further participation in this case due to her past relationship with Officer Glass."

In the ensuing days, Mary Anne Henry managed to raise Judge Schulz's ire with additional accusations that he considered "fairly outrageous." Because he was having trouble controlling his temper, he asked the court system to hire an attorney to deal with the state. Soon, his attorney approached him with a deal. If Schulz agreed to change venue and remove himself from the case, the state would agree to drop its complaints against him. Judge Schulz refused to take the deal.

He also wrote an opinion laying out his rationale.

"The court's law clerk functions as a confidential employee," Schulz wrote. "As such, the law clerk cannot reveal discussions that take place with the Court without violating the Oath of Office and Code of Professional Responsibility... the Court is neither able nor willing to assume that its former law clerk, Ms. Oechsli, would violate these obligations and disclose something to defense counsel or the state about the Court's 'thoughts and attitudes' concerning this case."

The final decision did not rest with Judge Schulz, however. Alaska law requires a disqualification request to go before another judge. Judge Victor D. Carlson handed down his decision two months later, noting that the facts in the case were not disputed. Cammy Oechsli had declared her romantic involvement with Phillip Weidner "soon after the mistrial was declared." That involvement "has apparently continued."

Carlson found it reasonable to assume that Oechsli had learned the "innermost thoughts of the judge" concerning the case and its participants. "The defense attorney [now] has an advantage over other counsel. This is unfair."

"It is ordered that the Honorable Thomas E. Schulz is disqualified for cause."

Even with a new judge in the offing, the next trial—if there was one—promised to be just as contentious. Mary Anne Henry, who had argued strongly for Ketchikan as the site of the first trial, was now opposed to that venue, asserting that an unbiased jury pool could not be found there. Phillip Weidner, who had insisted on a venue change for the first trial, asserting that an unbiased jury pool could not be found in Ketchikan, now favored keeping the trial there.[19]

The two sides could not agree on anything.

---

19   The decision to retry John Peel started out reasonably enough, but soon became a political football. To reach his decision, Alaska Attorney General Hal Brown spoke to both sides and the jury foreman—and sent the director of criminal prosecution to interview Larry Demmert. Brown reasoned that the case had turned on Demmert's credibility, and that credibility had been attacked relentlessly by the defense. The Demmert interview, which lasted almost a day, determined that the Libby 8 skipper was a trustworthy person. Based on the information they'd collected, Brown decided the state should retry John Peel. But Brown's boss, Governor Bill Sheffield, lost a primary challenge to fellow Democrat Steve Cowper. When Cowper won, a new Attorney General—Alaska pioneer Grace Berg Schaible—was tasked to review the Brown decision. Though urged on by defense counsel Phillip Weidner, Schaible found neither Weidner nor the Alaska criminal division to be much help in reaching a determination. After meeting with Hal Brown, and hearing his rationale for a retrial, Schaible made her decision; John Peel would be tried a second time.
    "It is my firm conviction that this case cannot be left hanging in an air of uncertainty," Schaible announced in a prepared statement. "It is the type of case that should be decided by a jury."

Part Three

On Third Street looking toward downtown Craig, Alaska, from the First Bank branch. At the end of the street is J.T. Brown, the dry-goods store where Dean Moon and John Peel bought rifles. Ruth Ann's restaurant is two doors down on the left. (Courtesy of Leland Hale.)

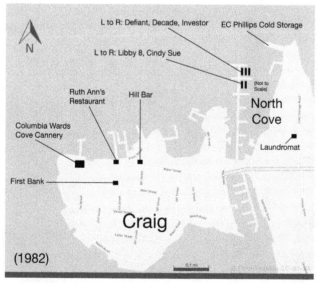

Map of downtown Craig, Alaska, with important landmarks. (Map data courtesy of OpenSeaMap (ODbl); illustration by Leland Hale.)

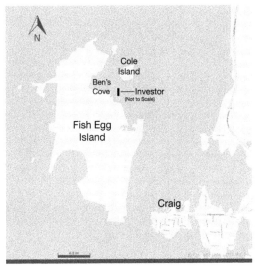

Map of Fish Egg Island in relation to Craig, Alaska. (Map data courtesy of OpenSeaMap (ODbl); illustration by Leland Hale)

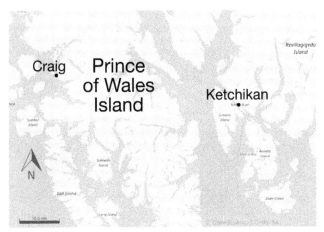

Map of Prince of Wales Island, Ketchikan and Craig. (Map data courtesy of OpenSeaMap (ODbl); illustration by Leland Hale.)

37

Juneau, Alaska
March - December 1987

From the water, Juneau looks like many a southeast Alaska town: the mountains rising straight from the water, the trees following until they reach solid rock. Some would say that her physical beauty is like no other, blessed as she is with two spectacular mountains looming over her shoulders like guardians. But Juneau is not like Ketchikan. Not like Craig. Not like Sitka or Wrangell or Petersburg or any of the other boroughs in Southeast Alaska. Juneau is unlike any other Alaskan city, for that matter, though she too was branded by the Gold Rush.

Juneau is a government town, with nearly half of her employment attributed to state, local and federal governments. Some Alaskans hate her because she seems remote from them, because the Alaska legislature is detached from the rest of the state. Despite those feelings, Alaskans never seem able to reject Juneau, even when presented with the opportunity to choose another capital.

When the second trial moved north, there was no escaping Juneau's identity. Many of the potential jurors worked for one government entity or another. Some of those selected worked for the government, though the defense had long made known its preference for blue-collar people, arguing that government workers would favor the state.

All of this put the newly appointed judge for *State v. Peel*, Juneau Superior Court Judge Walter L. "Bud" Carpeneti, in the midst a tsunami. Appointed to the Peel trial on March 6, he was quickly inundated by motions from both sides, each determined to make the most of Judge Schulz's absence. Then, with jury selection under way, and potential jurors gathered in the courthouse, Judge Carpeneti's in-court clerk came to him with a disturbing report.

Someone, she said, was in the foyer where potential jurors were waiting, complaining loudly that the defendant wasn't going to get a fair trial in Juneau. The jury, the man charged to everyone within earshot, wouldn't contain working people, but would have government employees predisposed to convict John Peel—in short, all of the defense's arguments. Judge Carpeneti immediately sent security out to make sure no one was talking about the case.

As the judge brought the first round of potential jurors in to meet the players for both sides, his in-court clerk spotted one of the defense investigators among them. She turned to Carpeneti and whispered, "that's the guy who was making all the statements earlier."

The judge's jury clerk confirmed that this was the same man she'd seen in the foyer. Judge Carpeneti was sufficiently concerned that he held an evidentiary hearing. Phillip Weidner, after talking to his defense investigator, insisted he was not the one who'd made the statements. When the in-court clerk took the stand, she described a man whose appearance and dress matched that of the defense investigator—and ID'd him in court as the culprit. Carpeneti's jury clerk did the same thing. Then the defense investigator took the stand and denied the charges, saying he was not there and didn't make the statements.

A deliberate, scholarly judge, even at the fairly young age of 42, Carpeneti resolved the dispute by saying that he could believe one person was mistaken in identifying the defense investigator. He found it difficult to believe that two people could reach the same conclusion independently of each other. The clerks, he decided, had accurately described the situation. Carpeneti issued a strong admonition to the defense investigator. "If there's even a hint of a repeat incident," he warned him, "you will be barred from this trial." The defense investigator continued to maintain his innocence.

Later on in jury selection, another revealing incident occurred. With the process dragging on into its second month, Phillip Weidner notified Judge Carpeneti that he had business to attend to in Anchorage and couldn't be there when the judge wanted to reconvene. Carpeneti tried to accommodate his schedule, but found he couldn't. Jury selection would continue the next day, at the time set by the judge.

The following day, Phil Weidner was not there at the appointed time. Judge Carpeneti insisted they go forward but Kenneth Callahan, the public defender who replaced the now gone Brant McGee, objected.

"You're here," Judge Carpeneti told him. "You're co-counsel. You've got to do it."

Fortunately for Kenneth Callahan, Phillip Weidner entered the courtroom before the public defender had to ask potential jurors any questions. But Weidner was outraged and incensed that they'd started without him. He approached the bench, still wearing his overcoat, and lodged a vigorous objection.

"You know," Judge Carpeneti told him, "defendant has co-counsel, that's what he's here for, the schedule's been set for a long time, and there wasn't sufficient reason to delay it. There's two attorneys on this side, and four on the other," Carpeneti reminded him, "and if I've got to recess the trial every time one of them says they can't be here, we're never gonna get it done."

Kenneth Callahan rarely uttered a word the rest of the way. The biggest difference during jury selection was the presence of one Josef Princiotta, a jury expert hired by the defense. With a beard, rose-tinted glasses, a handful of rings and long black hair tied in a ponytail, Princiotta looked like a refugee from a rock video. His claim to fame was his self-proclaimed ability to select juries solely on the basis of their physical characteristics. According to Princiotta, the most important part of a prospective juror's anatomy was his or her ears, the lobes of which represented the human head.

At this point, no turn in the *Investor* murder case seemed too strange or too bizarre to contemplate.

38

Juneau, Alaska
Friday, January 15, 1988 - Saturday, January 16, 1988

As John Peel's second trial began in Juneau's spacious federal courthouse, the room was packed. Judge Carpeneti had moved the trial to this courtroom to accommodate the extra spectators, although Juneau soon lost interest. The heart of this trial belonged to Ketchikan, and its soul belonged to Bellingham.

Even as the spectators thinned, however, the front of the courtroom was crammed. Not only had the exhibits crowded their way into the courtroom, so had the entire record of John Peel's first trial, stuffed into scores of banker's boxes. Both sides seemed determined to argue that the sheer volume of paper should allow their side to prevail.

In a change from the first trial, Henry's opening statement made several admissions. "The State can't tell you why that first shot was fired," she said, acknowledging that the state could not come up with a motive for the murders. Then she added that John Peel, "almost got away with it," itself an admission of how badly things had gone. More important to the prosecution's chances was the new evidence developed by her team. Henry confidently announced that all eight people on board the *Investor*—including Dean Moon—had been identified among the dead. The specter of Dean Moon, she was claiming, could now be vanquished once and for all.

The following day was Phillip Weidner's turn and, with the help of Josef Princiotta, he had come prepared. Princiotta set out before the jury eight wooden easels, each containing a portion of a time-line leading from the *Investor* murders, each also containing several terse captions.

Josef Princiotta's charts said things like:

MR. COULTHURST'S FINANCES ON THE BRINK.

THE POLICE AND PROSECUTION LET THE TRAIL GO COLD.

SERGEANT STOGSDILL SUBMITS HIS THEORY TO SOLVE THE CASE BY THE ONLY CONVENIENT METHOD FOR THE POLICE AND THE STATE.

STACKED DECK PHOTO LINEUP.

THE FIRST GRAND JURY INDICTMENT THROWN OUT.

NO NEW EVIDENCE FOR STATE.

At the break the prosecution had a complaint. The state hadn't seen the charts before and, not only were some of them "argumentative," but others violated the Court's protective orders. They demanded that the charts be covered up and the jury instructed to disregard them. Weidner insisted in counter-argument that the placards contained "relevant" information and were not argumentative.

Carpeneti hesitated. Wasn't "stacked deck" argumentative?

"If there is a problem on it, I guess we can white it out right now," Weidner replied. "I just want to address the jury."

Carpeneti pointed to other placards that seemed to violate the protective order, like the one that referred to Mark Coulthurst's finances being "on the brink." Weidner countered that the judge had ordered him "not to say his finances were illegal." In the end, the judge let the placards stay, noting that while they used "colorful language," that didn't make them objectionable.

By the time Weidner finished his opening statement, it was clear he had saved some of his strongest venom for Larry Demmert, whom he referred to as the state's "star witness." One of the placards read:

STATE LIES TO AND THREATENS LARRY DEMMERT. RESULT – DREAMS.

A second said:

> DEMMERT GIVES TESTIMONY WHICH REQUIRES PERJURY IMMUNITY.

Another said:

> LARRY DEMMERT, SCARED AND INFLUENCED BY HYPNOTIC DRUGS, AND THE THREAT OF JAIL, FLIP-FLOPS ON HIS STORY. CLAIMS TO SUDDENLY REMEMBER PEEL.

The defense attorney still had one more placard. He turned to it as he finished his opening statement. "January 1988," it read:

> WHERE DO WE GO FROM HERE?

Weidner provided his own answer, as he penned the words, "Not Guilty."

Josef Princiotta's placards were prophetic in at least one respect: they predicted the tone of the second trial. The first month was not much more than a continuous dispute, moderated with varying degrees of success by Judge Carpeneti. Although Mary Anne Henry had streamlined her witness list, and rearranged the order in which they appeared, Phillip Weidner stuck to a familiar line of attack.

When Henry led off with Sergeant Stogsdill, she was reverting to what had worked so well at both grand juries. When Phillip Weidner accused the trooper of failing to gather evidence at the crime scene, of not searching for fingerprints, of lying to witnesses, the grand jury and the press in his drive to arrest John Peel, he was repeating his criticisms from the first trial. The more things changed, the more things didn't change at all.

39

Juneau, Alaska
Wednesday, February 17, 1988 - Wednesday, April 20, 1988

The first month of the trial slogged through seemingly endless objections and forced jury breaks. On a typical day, the jury heard precious little testimony. During one of Larry Demmert's days on the stand, for example, only twenty minutes of testimony were taken. One day was lost because a juror was ill. Another day was lost because of a scheduled "jury day off." A third day was lost because it was a State holiday.

During Peel II, the jury was out of the courtroom as much as in. Judge Carpeneti tried to avoid sending the jury out, with little success. Carpeneti literally turned grey during the course of the trial. The impact of that endless shuffling was hard to gauge but, in this as any trial, the jury was trying to follow a story. Each time Carpeneti sent them out, he made it more difficult for them to follow that story. The trial was being chopped up into little pieces.

In a surprise turn of events, a new witness suddenly came forward to claim that he had heard John Peel's shipboard confession during the summer of 1983. Counsel for the state immediately sent Trooper Stogsdill to interview the man. It turned out there were two of them.

Charles and Walter Samuelson finally took the stand on Tuesday, February 23rd. They said they had met John Peel in 1983, while fishing near Kodiak, Alaska. Charles, the first brother to testify, said he was playing cribbage with Peel and mentioned having seen the burnt-out wreckage of the *Investor* while passing through Craig in 1982. Samuelson added that he hoped the murderer was arrested and executed for the crimes, perhaps unaware that Alaska lacked a death penalty.

"John looked at me and said, 'I did it. I killed them,'" Samuelson testified. He added, "He kind of had a weird smile," and named Mark Coulthurst and Dean Moon among his victims. Samuelson said he told Peel not to make such statements. He thought at the time that Peel was joking. The conversation came to an end, he added, when their boat had to be moved. Asked by newly added prosecutor Dean Guaneli why he hadn't spoken up about this incident, Charles Samuelson said his father "told me to keep my mouth shut."

When Phillip Weidner cross-examined Charles Samuelson, he hit him with everything he had. He noted that Charles was facing assault charges in Palmer, Alaska, as well as allegations that he furnished alcohol to minors when he initially approached the prosecution. Samuelson admitted he was on probation at the time these events occurred. Weidner further alleged that Samuelson had lied in past cases to avoid trouble, an allegation that Samuelson didn't deny.

Later that day, Walter Samuelson confirmed his brother's testimony. "He said he killed some people in Craig," the fisherman testified. "He said the *Investor* was the name of the boat. He said he burned it up."

Walter Samuelson insisted that Peel just said it once. On cross-examination, Walter Samuelson said he did not recall hearing Peel mention the names of Mark Coulthurst and Dean Moon. He said he didn't really believe Peel at the time and didn't want to hear any of it. He also said that he'd told his father he didn't think Peel was admitting to the crimes, that Peel's statement was "just bullshit, just a bunch of crap." He also admitted that his brother was worried about the assault charges hanging over his head. Walter Samuelson figured a deal was being made, although he didn't know of any deal.

Perhaps the most damaging testimony about the Samuelson brothers, however, came late in the trial, when their mother took the stand. She corroborated their claim that they'd kept quiet about Peel's confession on the advice of their father. Under questioning by Phil Weidner, she was asked about Charles Samuelson's immunity arrangement with the state.

"And isn't it true that he was very interested in getting those charges dismissed up there in Palmer—getting out of trouble?" Weidner asked her.

"Well, I think—no comment," Samuelson's mother replied. There was laughter from the jury box.

"Pardon me?" Weidner asked.

"No comment," the woman replied.

"No further questions," Weidner responded. "Thank you, ma'am."

Ruth Moon was the last witness for the prosecution. In emotional testimony, she told of hearing that people had died on the *Investor*, and hoping her son was alive. She fought back tears as she told of taking Dean Moon's dental records to the Coulthurst home, so troopers would have a way to identify the bodies. Moon also spoke of her unhappiness with the early investigation, when no one would tell her what had happened to her son.

"I just wanted them to be honest with me," she said. "I knew my son died on the boat."

When Ruth Moon left the stand, Mary Anne Henry moved to rest the prosecution's case. The time was 10:15 a.m., Monday, April 11, 1988. Phillip Weidner asked for a break. After the break, he was expected to call his initial witness, a former FBI fingerprint expert. When the court reconvened at 11:00, Judge Carpeneti asked Weidner, "Does the defendant have evidence to present?"

"Based upon the state of the evidence and the burden of proof," Weidner responded, "the defendant rests his case."

The jury was shocked. Mary Anne Henry and Bob Blasco were surprised. "There's no way the state can have any notice of that," Blasco said of Weidner's action once a recess was declared.

About the only people in the courtroom who were not taken aback by Weidner's apparently sudden strategy change were John Peel and his family. Even before Ruth Moon took the stand, Weidner had told his client he didn't intend to call any witnesses. That notice had come in a phone call during which a trembling John Peel said, "Okay."

After his surprise declaration, Phillip Weidner again made a motion for a judgment of acquittal. He said the state hadn't presented evidence proving John Peel committed the crimes. At the acquittal hearing the next day, both sides took their best shot. Judge Carpeneti denied Weidner's motion. It was time for each side to make their final statements to the jury.

By coincidence, Judge Schulz was in Juneau on business and he decided to drop in on the closing arguments. He wasn't in the courtroom long before the two sides argued and were summoned to a sidebar at the bench. Schulz thought to himself, "nothing much has changed."

Most striking was the way the two sides were arrayed. On the prosecution side was a battery of lawyers: Henry, Blasco, Gullufsen and newly added counsel, Dean Guaneli. On the defense side, Phillip Weidner sat alone with his client. For Schulz the symbolism of the message was clear: Phillip Weidner was single-handedly taking on the money and power of the state.

40

D ay one of jury deliberations went by without much of a peep from the jury. They asked the bailiff for exhibits as they needed them, but did not ask to listen to taped testimony. They were just getting started—but they were already busy.

All of the jurors had taken notes; one juror, a teacher, had filled a dozen secretarial binders. Using those notes, they took large sheets of butcher paper and started to outline the case on the wall. There were individual sheets for all the witnesses, individual sheets for all the major points of the case, individual sheets for the evidence. From that, they carved out what they regarded as important information from the witnesses and wrote that on another sheet. Each step of the way, they continued with their evaluation.

By the afternoon of day two, the walls were filled. The evaluation of witness testimony consumed much of the day. They were ready, they decided, for their first secret ballot. The forewoman counted the ballots and read the results. They had not reached a unanimous decision. They would continue with their deliberations.

For the rest of the day and all of the next, the jurors went over each of the witness statements and the entirety of the evidence. They reassessed everything they had heard. Everything they had seen. Everything they had written. On the third day, they finally asked to hear a tape from the trial. That tape was John Peel talking to the cops in Bellingham. They listened to the tape, and discussed it, but still didn't reach a decision. They decided instead to sleep on it, and discuss it again the following day.

On the fourth day, the jury did as they said they would. They returned to the evidence and spoke again of the witnesses. They dissected the prosecution case, analyzed the defense case, and took another vote. The time was 3:34 p.m. This time, the vote was unanimous. Forewoman Arlene Ryan told the bailiff they had reached a decision and soon all sides were on their way to the ninth floor of the Federal Courthouse in Juneau. If there was a surprise, it was that they had reached their decision so quickly.

Judge Carpeneti announced the jury's decision at 4:40 p.m. The tension in the room was palpable. After three and a half years and two trials, no one wanted to wait any longer. Judge Carpeneti didn't keep them waiting.

To the first count of murder, Judge Carpeneti announced, the jury had found John Kenneth Peel "not guilty." John Peel looked startled, but behind him applause was heard from his family and a shouted, "All right."

Peel's supporters turned quiet as the next eight "not guilty" verdicts were read. John Peel's astonishment turned to a smile. When Judge Carpeneti was finished, the Peel family and friends again broke into applause. Riding a tidal wave of emotion, John Peel broke into tears and had to be supported by Phillip Weidner. Soon, Peel traded his tears for hugs.

As the television cameras recorded John Peel's first moments as a free man, they could not conceal the joy on Cathy Peel's face. But John Peel did not look joyous, or happy, or even relieved. He looked surprisingly grim and tense. In a press conference held minutes after he left the courtroom, John Peel spoke to reporters for the first time.

"I'd just like to say it's terrible being innocent and being accused of a crime," he said. "This is a terrible thing for everyone to have to go through. It's been so many years," he said in a weary voice. Surrounded by reporters, friends, family and his attorneys, the 27-year-old thanked his supporters. "I was lucky to have so much support, so many people praying for me and standing behind me. Thank God it's over and justice did work this time."

John Peel was prevented from saying more when Phillip Weidner stepped in and cut him off. "It's an emotional situation," the defense attorney said. Both Peel and his wife, Cathy, refused to comment on their future plans.

"We're going to have no place to go but up from here," Cathy Peel predicted. But Phillip Weidner did most of the talking.

"Today is a wonderful day, not only for John Peel, but for justice in the state of Alaska," Phillip Weidner said. "The prosecutors have put an innocent man and his family through this ordeal for four years." The defense attorney pounded home the financial ruin both he and the Peel family had suffered, and said they were considering civil litigation to compensate for financial losses. Weidner did not hesitate to take one more swipe at the prosecution.

"From the moment it was issued, I have always said the indictment was not worth the paper it was written on," Weidner said. "I didn't put a case on because there was no need to dignify this case by putting on witnesses." As the press conference ended, Weidner put his arm around John Peel and hugged him. "I'm going down to the Red Dog to get a drink," he announced, referring to a local Gold Rush-style saloon with swinging doors and sawdust on the floor.

John Peel's mother, Marilyn, had another emotion entirely. After sitting through every day of the trial since its January inception, she later told reporters, "I'm sort of like a zombie. It's been three long days since the jury went out," she said, and then added, "It feels great because I have known from day one he was innocent."

As if seconding those words, the next day Phillip Weidner entered a motion demanding that the final judgment issued by Judge Carpeneti read, "Judgment of Innocence." He didn't get his wish. After Judge Carpeneti had his say, the judgment said what all such judgments say. Judgment of Acquittal.

In the ensuing days other voices were heard as well. Ruth Moon expressed her displeasure with the verdict. "Obviously I don't feel very good about it," she said. "I thought after being up there for a couple of weeks watching the trial, that they would find him guilty, as they should have."

The Coulthursts, meanwhile, were philosophical. "We have to basically now work with going on with our lives and put it all behind us," Sally Coulthurst noted. "Nothing will bring our children back and that's just the way it is."

"But we've got lots to live for," she added. "We have a wonderful new grandson, and I've still got two girls who are great and the greatest husband and me. There are a lot of things to be thankful for," Coulthurst noted, among them the determined efforts of the police and prosecutors.

"They worked hard," Sally Coulthurst said. "They went all-out."

Mary Anne Henry, meanwhile, expressed her disappointment in the verdict, while defending the judicial system that produced it. "Our system is built on the theory that it is better to let nine guilty persons go free than convict one innocent man. In this case, John Peel is going free for nine crimes," Henry proclaimed.

The prosecutor further revealed that the state would not pursue a new investigation of the *Investor* murders, even as she admitted to reporters that she was unsurprised by the verdicts. She had interviewed three of the alternate jurors who were excused before the start of deliberations; she got the feeling the state would lose the case. Henry added that evidence the state was prevented from presenting to the jury might have resulted in a different outcome.

"It's hard to predict how that would have affected the jury's decision," she noted.

"Apparently, the state did not have sufficient evidence to convince the jury beyond a reasonable doubt," she added. "It has not affected the state's view. The state knows who the killer is."

41

When Judge Walter Carpeneti lifted the gag order that bound the trial participants to silence, jurors both past and present started to speak out. Ex-jury foreman Heidi Ekstrand, by now a former *Ketchikan Daily News* Managing Editor, told the *Ketchikan Daily News* that jurors in the first trial "listened to the same witnesses, received the same instructions from the judge and came to completely different conclusions."

Some of the jurors at the first trial were open to discussion, she said; others had already reached a decision; nothing could move them closer to agreement. They voted four guilty and eight not guilty on the seven murder charges that excluded Dean Moon—and three guilty and nine not guilty in the murder of Moon.

Eckstrand tried to place her own feelings within the context of those deliberations. "I was among a few jurors who 'believed' or had 'a feeling' Peel was guilty, yet still we voted innocent because we couldn't find enough good evidence to support our feelings. Do I vote according to my feelings, or according to the evidence presented in court? The judge's instructions were clear: we were to try the issues solely on the evidence introduced. It was a tough struggle then and remains the issue I have to live with."

For the jurors at the second trial everything seemed to boil down to the way the state presented its case, and the mistakes made by the Alaska State Troopers. In a 1988 piece by Peter Carbonara in *The American Lawyer*, jurors showed their frustration. "They didn't show me anything that would allow me to put a man away for the rest of his life," said juror Ron Hilbert of the prosecution case.

"If there was a case against John Peel to start with," added juror Geraldine Alps, "the Alaska State Troopers and prosecutors blew it."

But jurors couldn't agree on what made the biggest difference in their decision. One juror told Carbonara that evidence of Peel's fingerprints on the *Investor* would have turned the case around. Another said the state's inability to establish a credible motive presented a major problem for jurors. Arlene Ryan, jury forewoman at the second trial, said the lack of a positive identification of Peel as the skiffman played a considerable role.

"There were always just resemblances and similarities," Ryan said. "No one would finger him."

A crucial moment in jury deliberations during the second trial came after they listened to the Peel interview tape. Although they did not hear the entire interview—parts of it constituted evidence that Mary Anne Henry could not present at trial—the jury was convinced that John Peel had not said what Mary Anne Henry said he did. Based on that tape all the undecided jurors changed their vote to "not guilty." They believed that John Peel was a scared young man who was being hounded by police, although at least one juror wondered: "How does a mass killer act?"

Facts and evidence aside, the personalities arrayed before them at trial sometimes overwhelmed everything else. One of the jurors at the first trial drew pictures of the proceedings. One was a drawing of Phillip Weidner, looking like Abraham Lincoln in a log cabin. Many of the jurors at the second trial told Carbonara that Phillip Weidner egged on the prosecution—and that the prosecution had fallen for it. Or at least Mary Anne Henry and Bob Blasco had fallen for it. The jurors weren't impressed.

Second trial juror Geraldine Alps summed things up by noting that some jurors thought the state had sent in kids to make the case against John Peel. They didn't like the case the state presented and they didn't like the way Henry and Blasco presented themselves. Many were the days, alternate juror Phillip Smith noted, when Henry seemed to let her emotions get the best of her. They saw deputy district attorney Bob Blasco as a strident man whose dominant tone was one of whiny exasperation. Weidner seemed able to goad Blasco into endless objections, which were eventually met by audible groans from the jury.

One juror started whispering, "Oh noooo, Mr. Bob!" whenever Blasco stood to speak, imitating the infamous *Saturday Night Live* puppet.

Brant McGee was even more forceful in his description of the prosecution. "They hated our guts," he noted in *The American Lawyer* article. "There was a feeling of deep personal hostility."

Yet even McGee admitted that Phillip Weidner could try his patience. "I would just grit my teeth over some of the thing's he'd try," McGee admitted. "But goddamn if he didn't win."

In the fall of 1988, the *Investor* murders were featured on the TV news magazine *A Current Affair*. The show featured John Peel, triangulated with interviews of Mary Anne Henry and Mark Coulthurst's parents, John and Sally. After a soft opening that showed John and Cathy Peel in a park with their young son, the program turned to harder truths.

The Coulthursts reiterated their belief that John Peel was responsible for killing Mark, his family and the *Investor* crew. Sally Coulthurst told interviewer David Lee Miller that, "I really think he [Peel] just freaked out and did it… 'Cause he was jealous of Mark. Jealous of the boat and mad that he was fired from the boat."

Mary Anne Henry was asked whether John Peel committed, "the perfect crime, the murder of eight people."

She responded in characteristically tight-lipped fashion: "No, I wouldn't say that he committed the perfect crime. Because committing the perfect crime would mean that he would never have been found out. I also don't think that he beat the system. The system simply worked."

"But if the system worked," Miller asked, "wouldn't John Peel be in prison?"

"No. Not necessarily," Henry replied. "Because, again, the system also accounts for the fact that it's better to let certain guilty people go free than to convict an innocent person. And, as a result of that, we are required to have sufficient evidence to convince a jury beyond a reasonable doubt. In this case, apparently, we did not have sufficient evidence."

John Peel got the last word. Asked how he would respond to these accusations, he answered, "The same thing I'd say to anybody. I didn't do it, you know, I'm not guilty, I didn't have anything to do with it. That's the bottom line. I did not do it. I'm just, you know, grateful to everybody and the Lord, that the jury saw that."

"What is it going to take to clear your name completely?" Miller wondered.

"For them to solve the case. You know, to find the people or person that did this, that committed this crime. That's the only thing that can clear my name," Peel told him.

"Think they will?" Miller asked.

"I don't... I think Mary Anne said they weren't investigating any further. You know, in her mind, she knows who did it."

"You did."

"That's in her mind, yeah," John Peel responded. "So, you know... If... You know, if we had the resources... I'd... If I had the resources I'd reopen the investigation, you know... "

"So this thing's never gonna go away..."

"No, apparently not," Peel responded, with resignation in his voice. "Only time will tell."

Two years later, Phillip Paul Weidner filed a civil suit on John Peel's behalf. By then, Peel's parents were living in a small Bellingham apartment, after losing their home in John's defense. John was living in a trailer court.

Weidner's complaint noted that John Peel "was arrested one day after the first birthday of his infant son." He added that Peel was "subjected to public ridicule and humiliation, emotional distress, mental suffering and anguish," "loss of an opportunity to bond with his infant son," and "loss of wages and opportunity to support his family." Weidner added that John Peel "continues to suffer damages and will suffer damages in the future, and he and his family will continue to suffer for the rest of their lives as a result of the actions of the defendants herein."

In court documents, Weidner based his wrongful-prosecution claim in part on an eight-page trooper memo written in 1984, two years after the Labor Day weekend slayings. The memo, by Sgt. James Stogsdill, was the one that named Peel as the key suspect but said there was "no case" without a confession and supporting evidence.

The suit asked $100 million in compensatory damages for John Peel and an additional $25 million for his wife, Catherine. It also demanded $20 million for their son, Kenneth, $10 million for each of John Peel's parents and another $5 million each for his sister and brother-in-law. Add to that the $2 million for attorney fees, plus the costs associated with John Peel's criminal defense, and they were asking for $177 million.

Named in the lawsuit were fifteen individuals or entities. Collectively they seemed to represent every phase of John Peel's arrest and trial. The State of Alaska was named. Mary Anne Henry was named. The City of Bellingham was named, and was its Police Department and Detective Dave McNeill. Then there were the Alaska State Troopers, both as an organization and as individuals, with Jim Stogsdill, Roy Holland, John Glass and Glenn Flothe called out specifically.

The grounds of the civil suit were as wide-ranging as the people it named. The defendants were charged with false arrest, abuse of process, malicious prosecution, breach of fiduciary duty and interference with constitutional rights. The lawsuit also charged the defendants with false imprisonment, conspiracy, denial of a right to a fair and impartial grand jury, and witness intimidation. In all, 24 claims were made against the named defendants, including unethical conduct for the Larry Demmert incident during which Valium was allegedly obtained "at the request and with aid" of the defendants.

The suit singled out Mary Anne Henry for "libel and slander" because she made "statements to the effect that Mr. Peel was 'guilty,' notwithstanding the acquittal, and that the Alaska State Troopers and she knew that he was 'guilty.' " Henry was also cited for "legal malpractice" because she allegedly "failed to properly supervise and evaluate evidence being presented to the State of Alaska by Trooper John Glass, due to her romantic relationship with Mr. Glass."

John Peel's civil suit against the State of Alaska was finally settled and approved by federal Judge H. Russel Holland on October 24, 1997, seven years after it was filed. The negotiated settlement ended more than a decade of court proceedings, but shed no light on what happened in Craig. John Peel received $900,000 from the State of Alaska—far less than the $177 million originally sought.

Daniel Gerety, an Anchorage lawyer who represented the state, confirmed the case had been settled. Both Gerety and Phillip Weidner declined comment beyond a prepared statement saying the state had agreed to pay damages without acknowledging wrongdoing.

"This was a compromise settlement," the statement said. "John Kenneth Peel and his family have decided to avoid the expense, emotional drain and effort of further civil litigation."

After fifteen years, millions of dollars, a seemingly endless investigation and two highly contentious trials, the John Peel case had finally run its course. Despite the best efforts of all parties involved, the entire affair trickled away with barely a murmur. The investigation was never reopened. No one was any happier. No one was any wiser. Nobody won.

Epilogue

Seattle, Washington, May 2017

Even as the civil suit was filed, many of the principals in the *Investor* trial had already moved on. Between the first and second trials, Mary Anne Henry requested a transfer from Ketchikan back to Anchorage, where her prosecutor's career had begun.

"I asked for a demotion," she told a reporter for *The American Lawyer*, "so I wouldn't have to think about anything but the Peel trial." She admitted that the move derailed her career.

After the trial, Henry bounced around in various criminal justice system capacities. She took on an active role as Assistant District Attorney in Anchorage; by 2002, Henry was supervising the Anchorage violent crimes unit. But Henry's health problems—she had long suffered from asthma—began to incapacitate her. In 2002, she delivered the opening statement in a high-profile murder case against 22-year-old Joshua Wade, but a bout of pneumonia forced her to withdraw and return to her duties as head of the violent crimes unit.

By 2004, Henry's career had taken another turn. She was named as a temporary replacement for a judge who died while on a hunting trip. Two years later, she was appointed to head the Alaska Office of Victim's Rights. She lasted a year before being named Deputy Director of the Department of Law's criminal division. Henry retired from that post two months later. She died in Portland, Oregon, in 2011, at the age of 59, her death attributed to liver failure due to chronic hepatitis.

Bob Blasco, Henry's co-counsel through both Peel trials, left the prosecutor's office. He moved to private practice with a Juneau law firm. Patrick Gullufsen eventually joined the Attorney General's office, serving as deputy attorney general for the Criminal Division, before becoming the Juneau district attorney. He retired in 2010 after serving as the Alaska Department of Law's cold case prosecutor for three years. In 2013, the Alaska Supreme Court suspended Gullufsen's law license for eighteen months at the request of the Alaska Bar Association. The suspension originated from a 2010 case in which Gullufsen withheld the results of a DNA test from an accused murderer's defense attorneys and the court. Gullufsen did not dispute the ruling, adding that he had been fighting leukemia and was overly fatigued during the trial.

Brant McGee, meanwhile, continued the public advocacy role he took on in 1984. After retiring from the Office of Public Advocacy in 2004, he studied human rights law at Columbia Law School, served in Afghanistan as advisor to the public defender office established by the International Legal Foundation and worked for the Environmental Defender Law Center. He also competed in (and won) the Alaska Mountain Wilderness Classic. Not once. Three times. He finally quit when he realized he couldn't deal with the sleep deprivation required to win.

In 1993, Phillip Weidner paid $1,500 in sanctions resulting from the two Peel trials. He paid them under protest, after losing appeals that went all the way to the Alaska Supreme Court. At least he had company; the state paid sanctions as well. His highest fines resulted from asserting that Mark Coulthurst was a major cocaine dealer during closing statements at the first trial—even though Judge Schulz had ordered him not to—and from calling Larry Demmert an addict, even though Judge Carpeneti had ordered him not to. Both incidents seemed to prove the assertion that Phillip Weidner didn't much care what judges thought of him. He continues to take on cases that put him on the side of the "little guy" and against the power of major corporations and the government.

The Alaska State Troopers involved in the *Investor* case went their separate ways. Trooper Anderson left the troopers in 1989 and built a fishing lodge in Klawock. Sergeants Holland and Miller retired, the latter to work for a private security firm. Sergeant Stogsdill left the troopers in 1993 and started a guide service on the Kenai Peninsula. He couldn't stay away from law enforcement; he joined the Alaska

Bureau of Investigation's cold case investigation unit in 2002, where he helped break a number of unsolved murders.

Sergeant Flothe was promoted to lieutenant, his life ever more consumed with administrivia, before he too retired from the troopers. He played an advisory role on the movie, "The Frozen Ground," based on the Robert Hansen murders in Anchorage. Jerry Mackie, the young man who first spotted John Peel, went on to represent the district of Craig in the Alaska State Legislature, first as a House member, later as a Senator. He more recently owned a "governmental relations" firm engaged in lobbying the Alaska Legislature.

Judge Schulz—after a long career on the bench—retired in 1992 and took a graduate degree in pastoral ministry, hoping to ply his newly acquired skills in his Ketchikan parish. A change in bishops put those plans on hold and Schulz moved with his wife to California— only to return to Alaska, his first love. In 2014, the Ketchikan Chamber of Commerce named Judge Schulz and his wife, Mary, Citizens of the Year for their combined record of community service. In accepting the award, Judge Schulz said, "I came down here from Juneau in '73, and all I wanted to be was a trial judge. I found a great community." The *Investor* case remains the most trying of his career.

Cammy Oechsli, the former assistant of judge Schulz, married a fellow attorney named Scott Taylor and, as Camille Oechsli Taylor, took a position as a Public Member Commissioner for the Alaska Oil and Gas Conservation commission, serving from 1997 to 2003. She was succeeded in her post by Sarah Palin.

In 1998, Judge Carpeneti was appointed to the Alaska Supreme Court—a tribute to his judicial skills. He served as the Chief Justice of the Alaska Supreme Court from 2009 to 2012, with some of his decisions trailing into early 2013. On more than one occasion, Phillip Weidner came before him and the other justices. The state of Alaska is still an overgrown small-town.

As for Larry Demmert, he pursued multiple opportunities in the fishing industry, including one as President of Tlingit Ocean Fisheries. He also lent his memories to "Angels to Ashes," a chronicle of the *Investor* murders that alleges the murders were drug-related. *Libby 8* crewmember Brian Polinkus, meanwhile, continued in the maritime industry, eventually becoming a tugboat captain.

Only a year passed before some of the Peel alumnae found themselves involved in another infamous case, this one the 1989 Exxon Valdez disaster. As Anchorage Assistant District Attorney, Mary Anne Henry brought the case of Exxon Valdez Capt. Joseph Hazelwood before a grand jury. After hearing charges that, among other things, Hazelwood had been drinking and had left the bridge to an unqualified third mate, the grand jury returned several felony indictments against Hazelwood.

Sgt. Jim Stogsdill had the role of protecting Hazelwood during his court appearances, even as he worked as a prosecution investigator in the oil spill. In 1990, a judge refused to let Stogsdill testify to "small talk" he'd had with Hazelwood, in which Hazelwood had referred to a Valdez drinking buddy that some called a "ghost companion," because he'd never turned up after the incident.

And then there was Jim Robinson, the former owner of Craig Auto, who made a spectacular name for himself after his abortive role in the first Peel trial. As chronicled by the *Anchorage Daily News*, when the Exxon Valdez ran into Bligh Reef, and Exxon began chartering boats as clean up vessels, Jim Robinson pounced, first by wrangling charter contracts and then buying boats to fulfill the contracts.

Robinson's business ethics were highly suspect; there were allegations that he bribed an Exxon contract official with "money, ivory, a fur coat, and the services of a prostitute" to get cleanup contracts. Exxon further charged that Robinson "claimed to own boats he didn't own, lied about their capabilities and size, and falsified logs and invoices to get paid." Exxon filed a civil action in 1990, seeking $2.5 million in damages. Even after the Exxon Valdez allegations, Robinson stayed in the boat chartering business. His shady practices ultimately led to tragedy on remote Seguan Island in the Aleutian Islands.

A vessel owned by Robinson, the *Red Jacket*, was towing a barge slated to pick up construction equipment on Atka Island, the last Native village in the Aleutian chain. But the *Red Jacket* was not a tug, the barge had a crack in its hull and fall storms were approaching with a vengeance. Things quickly went south. The barge broke its line, not once but several times; the *Red Jacket* ultimately lost the barge entirely. The *Red Jacket's* fresh water tank was also breached and the skipper sent two crewmen to Seguam Island to get fresh water. During the night it snowed and the *Red Jacket* crew lost sight of the two men. By morning, their inflatable boat was gone and so were all traces of the men. A coroner's jury declared them dead in March 1991; no criminal charges were filed in that incident.

By 1992, Robinson had been charged by the State of Alaska with bribery and fraud related to cleanup contracts he secured during the Exxon Valdez oil spill. In March of 1994, Robinson pleaded no contest to charges he bribed an Exxon official and submitted fake bills for cleanup work. In February of 1995, the 52-year-old Robinson was sentenced to a four-year jail term for defrauding Exxon.

Robinson's habit of leaving destruction in his wake was near perfect.

In an ironic development, Ruth Ann's restaurant in Craig—the site of the Coulthurst's last supper—burned down in December 2015. No criminal actions were suspected, but the restaurant was a Craig landmark and its loss was deeply felt.

The Coulthurst family remains convinced that John Peel murdered their family and all the crew on the *Investor*. Nothing, not even his acquittal, could temper those feelings. In 1992, on the ten-year anniversary of the murders, they confessed to feeling a decade of grief. They told *Bellingham Herald* reporter Trask Tapperson that they planned to spend the anniversary weekend at a British Columbia RV park.

"We'll enjoy ourselves—and try to forget," Sally Coulthurst told him. She had a hard time doing so. "I've got the kids' pictures by my bed, so I see them every day," she said.

John Coulthurst, who died in 2010 at the age of 77, admitted at the time of the ten-year anniversary that there were some days "that I don't think about it." He later told this author that he held a begrudging respect for Phillip Weidner. "If I was ever arrested for murder," the senior Coulthurst once mused, "I'd want Weidner for my lawyer."

Daughter Laurie Coulthurst Hart, meanwhile, keeps her family's memory alive by memorializing them each year at the Blaine, Washington, blessing of the fleet.

After his acquittal, John Peel returned to work as a laborer. He continues to proclaim his innocence, aware that some people will never hold him guiltless. His has not been an easy path.

After his lawsuit was settled, John Peel and his wife bought a two-story house with acreage in Ferndale, a suburban neighborhood north of Bellingham. Within two years, the couple was divorced; ex-wife Cathy got the house. In the following years, court records reveal that John Peel was convicted of several felonies, all related to prescription drugs. Peel has not been involved with the criminal justice system since 2003. He is currently employed as a skilled welder at the Ferndale oil refinery and has become good friends with Brian Keown, the older brother of *Investor* victim Jerome Keown.

The *Investor* tragedy remains unsolved.

Acknowledgements

The author would like to thank the following people and institutions for their support and assistance during the arduous journey *What Happened in Craig*, took from first draft in 1992 to final publication: Major Walter Gilmour, AST, Retired; Col. Tom Anderson, AST, Retired, and FOAST; Mary Anne Henry; Alaska State Troopers Sgt. Chuck Miller and Bob Anderson; Jerry Mackie and the residents of Craig, Alaska; Sally and John Coulthurst; Lisa Coulthurst; Roy Tussing; Erling Carlson and the crew of *F/V Three Sisters*; Kim Hammer; Judge Thomas Schulz; Marcia Hilley; Ron Hilbert; Larry Hibpshman and the staff at the Alaska State Archives in Juneau; the staff at the University of Washington Microform & Newspapers desk; the staff at the University of Washington Gallagher Law Library; Sheila Toomey; *Fisherman's Journal*; Eric Thomas, Donald Tapperson, Trask Tapperson and other photographers and reporters at the *Bellingham Herald*; Hall Anderson, David S. Kiffer, Gregg Poppen and other reporters and photographers at the *Ketchikan Daily News*; the *Anchorage Daily News*; the *Juneau Empire*; Sue Cross and the *Associated Press*; Doug McNair and *Pacific Fishing* magazine; Grace Berg Schaible and her biographer, Donna C. Willard-Jones; *People Magazine*; *The New York Times*; *KJUD TV*; *A Current Affair*; the *Anchorage Dispatch News*; the *Seattle Times*; Peter Carbonara and *The American Lawyer*; Brian Keown; Christine Barnett; Fred Bowman; Lorraine Miller; John McKay and the inimitable Lael Morgan.